FROM:

_____

TO:

_____

DATE:

_____

PRAISE FOR *COZY WHITE COTTAGE SEASONS*

"Liz is the epitome of authenticity and genuine enthusiasm. While her beautiful aesthetic and effortless style are admirable, her peppy, optimistic personality instantly draws you in. Her content is escapism at its finest and her family, farm, and overall lifestyle all serve as inspiration for so many people, including myself. The pages of this book will bring endless joy and bright smiles to faces everywhere, just like Liz, Jose, and Cope do."

—**BRIAN PATRICK FLYNN**, HOST OF *HGTV DREAM HOME*, *HGTV URBAN OASIS*, AND MAGNOLIA NETWORK'S *MIND FOR DESIGN*

"Liz's tips are doable and fun and when implemented achieve so much cozy! The book will not only be on my coffee table but will be referenced season after season."

—**JEAN STOFFER**, JEAN STOFFER DESIGN AND STOFFER HOME IN GRAND RAPIDS, MICHIGAN

"*Cozy White Cottage Seasons* is such a beautiful example of what Liz Marie does best— create and generously share ideas to implement in your home and life. She is one of the most prolific creatives I know and the abundance of talent and enthusiasm that radiate from her is all over these pages—and it's infectious. As you browse through the chapters, you will find yourself flush with inspiration, brimming with ideas, and anticipating the change of each season."

—**MARIAN PARSONS**, AUTHOR OF *FEELS LIKE HOME* AND THE BLOG *MISS MUSTARD SEED*

"Liz's blog is the epitome of cozy farmhouse living and her book will be a must-read for those of us who admire her chic, modern farmhouse style, and who love to celebrate seasonal living to the fullest. What stands out in this book is Liz's big heart, and her words read like a warm and welcoming hug at a time when we need it most."

—**PAULA SUTTON**, WRITER, STYLIST, BLOGGER, AND AUTHOR OF *HILL HOUSE LIVING: THE ART OF CREATING A JOYFUL LIFE*

COZY *white* COTTAGE

Seasons

100 WAYS TO BE COZY ALL YEAR LONG

LIZ MARIE
· GALVAN ·

PHOTOGRAPHY BY ANNA VANDERBERG

THOMAS NELSON
Since 1798

Published in Nashville, Tennessee, by Thomas Nelson. Thomas Nelson is a registered trademark of HarperCollins Christian Publishing, Inc.

Images used under license from Anna Vandenberg. Additional photography by Liz Marie Galvan.

Written with the assistance of Tama Fortner, represented by Cyle Young of C.Y.L.E. (Cyle Young Literary Elite, LLC), a literary agency.

Thomas Nelson titles may be purchased in bulk for educational, business, fundraising, or sales promotional use. For information, please email SpecialMarkets@ThomasNelson.com.

Any internet addresses, phone numbers, or company or product information printed in this book are offered as a resource and are not intended in any way to be or to imply an endorsement by Thomas Nelson, nor does Thomas Nelson vouch for the existence, content, or services of these sites, phone numbers, companies, or products beyond the life of this book.

ISBN 978-1-4002-2457-9 (eBook)
ISBN 978-1-4002-2455-5 (Hardcover)

Printed in United States

21 22 23 24 25 LSC 10 9 8 7 6 5 4 3 2 1

To my husband, Jose, and my son, Copeland Beau—
thank you for being my light, even on the darkest of days.

CONTENTS

CONTENTS

INTRODUCTION

ozy. It's become so much more than a word for me, so much more than a way to decorate and design. It is now a way of life, of approaching the world and the choices we make within it. These days, especially, I find that coziness is less about paint colors, linens, and lighting—though I could talk for days about those things. Instead, cozy is more about creating a space that welcomes, nourishes, and surrounds us with warmth, love, and comfort through each changing season of the year and the ever-changing seasons of our lives. Cozy is about transforming our own little corner of the world into a private refuge. Not a place of perfection, but a place of peace and belonging, a place to retreat to when all the demands and distractions of life press in.

But how do we do that? How do we create that sanctuary for ourselves and those we share this life with? That's a question I began asking myself a few years ago. Though I have been drawn to decorating and design since I was a child (thanks to the classiest woman I've ever met—my grandmother), it wasn't until after I married that I began to intentionally cultivate this cozy approach to life. Jose was in the military, and the day after we were married, we were relocated to North Carolina. With friends and family far away and a husband who deployed for months at a time, I searched for a sense of security and comfort. Adding cozy cottage touches to our small rental and trying out some DIY projects brought me joy and reminders of home in a new, unfamiliar place.

A blog, a book, and a baby later, Jose, Cope, and I are now back in our home state of Michigan, living in our forever home—a hundred-year-old farmhouse perched in the middle of eight sprawling acres. We call it White Cottage Farm, and it's an ever-evolving work in progress. We're filling the grounds with orchards and gardens, sheep, cats, dogs,

and even bees. We're filling our home with DIYs and cozy cottage style, and our hearts are already filled to overflowing with our son, Copeland Beau—affectionately known as Cope. Through my own imperfections I share that life doesn't have to be perfect to be cozy.

Perhaps you've known me for a while through my posts at LizMarieBlog.com, or perhaps you met me through my first book, *Cozy White Cottage,* or maybe this is our introduction as you are just now beginning to seek out a cozier way to live. Regardless, let me say, "Welcome." Here you'll find ideas and inspiration for making your own home a haven of coziness in every season of the year—whether it's a high-rise apartment in the city, a tiny house in the suburbs, or a hundred-year-old house on a farm.

In my first book, we explored a hundred different ways to cozy up your home and décor. But in *Cozy White Cottage Seasons* I'm inviting you to journey with me through an entire year of coziness. Together, we'll create spaces, places, and moments of coziness that draw out the best of each of the seasons. Whether you're savoring the fresh air of spring, the vibrant and joyful colors of summer, the ever-changing wonders of fall, or the wrapped-up-in-blankets warmth of winter, each season beckons with its own brand of coziness, and I'll show you how to bring that out in your décor. We'll also talk through some of the basics of design and how to adapt them for the different times of year. But more than that, we'll look at how to make the most of each season, weaving a thread of coziness throughout the different facets of our lives, as well as in our homes.

And of course, the holidays. From the freshness of Easter to the fireworks of summer, from the crackling fires of fall to the coziness of Christmas, the holidays offer so many opportunities to create, to dream, to design, and to decorate. More than that, though, they encourage us to make sweet memories with those we love.

Beyond those special days, there's an everyday cozy that ebbs and flows with the seasons, always present yet ever shifting in subtle and not-so-subtle ways as we rearrange and refresh those foundational elements of our homes. Whatever the day or season might be, I believe coziness should involve all five of our senses. That means incorporating layers and textures to touch, colors and patterns to capture our vision, smells to awaken minds and memories, tastes to savor, and sounds that become the playlist for our lives.

As we set about the process of making our homes cozy, we create a much-needed refuge from the world and its craziness. Now more than ever I believe that tranquility within our homes inspires tranquility within our souls. And don't we all long for a bit more peace in our lives?

So grab a cup of your favorite soothing beverage, and find a quiet place to read, reflect, and dream. Kick off your shoes and curl up with a pillow and a soft throw . . . and let's take a cozy trip through the seasons together.

SPRING

SPRING

I absolutely love spring. Because I live in a state with long, cold winters, the anticipation of spring makes its arrival so much sweeter. It's that time of year when everything is fresh and new, bursting with promise and possibility. By the time spring finally shows up, I'm ready to shake off the layers of winter and throw open the windows to enjoy the warm sunshine and sweet breezes that make our home and our souls feel new again. The garden calls my name with the rich, dark scent of freshly turned soil, ready for planting, nurturing, and tending. I'm more than ready to make mud pies with my son and watch as he runs through the grass and chases the spring lambs.

Because returning to the outdoors in spring brings me so much joy, it's important to me to bring that freshness into our home as well. Touches of greenery get tucked in everywhere—on bookshelves, tables, counters, and corners. Sprays of flowering branches spill out of buckets, baskets, and market bags. Windows are opened, a deep cleaning happens, and the line between outside and inside is wonderfully blurred, giving everything a "welcome to our garden" feel. It's the cozy of springtime. Warm, light, and airy—and welcoming us in.

SEASONAL CHECKLIST

I love Mondays, mornings, and changes of season because these are opportunities to start fresh and begin something new. The transition from one season to the next is the perfect time to make changes, start new projects, and refresh your space. If you already have a good momentum for your seasonal changes, keep going with that. If you are struggling or in a rut, use this time to press the reset button!

This is a great list to get started in any season, as many of the things I do repeat during each seasonal change. If you ever need assistance with your transition from one season to the next, refer back to this list for help!

SEASONAL CHECKLIST

Freshen up the whole house with a thorough cleaning, tackling just one room or space at a time. (See page 31 for a full cleaning inventory.)			
Repaint or freshen up paint in any rooms that may need it or where you are craving a new look. Don't forget—paint includes ceilings, floors, walls, cabinets, doors, and furniture!			
Remove any greenery that doesn't work for this season and add in new greenery or houseplants that do.			
Exchange blankets, throws, and bed linens for lighter ones in the spring and summer months and thicker ones in the fall and winter.			
Consider switching out seasonal pillows, window treatments, and rugs for lighter textures.			
Swap out candles and scents to match the season.			
Create a seasonal centerpiece for your table or kitchen island.			
Update porch, patio, and outdoor areas—one space at a time.			
Change out the front door décor.			
Switch up the artwork throughout your home.			
Don't forget to update tea towels hanging in your kitchen.			

No. 01

RECEIVED BY

SPRING DÉCOR STAPLES

There's just something about shifting from the chill of winter to the welcoming warmth of spring that feeds my soul. It's a time to clear away clutter and open ourselves to the promise of new beginnings.

In our home, the transition to the new season is a gradual and unhurried process. Room by room, winter layers are lifted up and assessed, then either purged or packed away. And room by room, we clean, making everything as fresh as the new season. Gradually, we bring in touches of springtime décor.

I love to add a touch here and there, giving a gentle nod to springtime. I add to, remove, replace, and rearrange as I have a moment day to day. The process is both grounding and soothing. And while I believe "style" is something that is ever evolving, there is a handful of staples that I find myself returning to again and again as I seek to bring the outdoor beauty of spring into our home.

* **Houseplants and greens:** From pothos to topiaries to angel vine to cypress trees, I'm happiest when there's a touch of green in every corner of our home. I put greens in all sorts of containers—baskets, buckets, bags, and bowls. Faux or real, greens add color, light, and freshness to every space.

* **Linens:** Light, slightly wrinkled linens, faded florals, and pillows made from antique textiles add coziness without being too heavy.

* **All things garden:** Antique garden tools, watering cans, and pretty seed packets—gather and use them to create homey vignettes on mantels, tabletops, and shelves. Layer terracotta pots, especially those coated with moss or an antique patina, for a greenhouse touch.

* **Architectural salvage:** Chippy white corbels, old windows, or any

architectural salvage adds the perfect hint of an old-world garden and creates a beautiful backdrop for spring vignettes.

❦ Baskets, bags, and buckets: Containers, especially when filled to the brim with plants and stems, instantly amp up spring décor. Tuck one into a corner, add them to shelves and tabletops, or hang one on a wall for instant warmth and depth.

❦ Utilitarian items: My household essentials are all aesthetically pleasing, allowing me to display these items throughout our home as décor. Consider replacing your household essentials (brooms, dustpans, scissors, dryer balls, etc.) when needed for more aesthetically pleasing items you feel comfortable displaying in your home. It makes cleaning more attainable for my busy lifestyle to have these items out as a reminder!

SPRING WARDROBE STAPLES

By the time spring strolls into Michigan, I'm ready to pack away the heavy clothes of winter. Warmer temperatures call for lighter colors and textures, but still-chilly mornings and evenings mean layers are a must.

I believe it's just as important to feel cozy and comfortable in our own clothes. Here are some of my favorite wardrobe pieces for spring:

- **Button-up blouse:** Roll up the sleeves and pair with jeans for the ultimate cool, casual vibe. Or wear with a skirt or pants and add an eye-catching necklace for a dressier look.
- **Cardigans:** Layer over tees and blouses on chilly mornings and cool evenings for an extra bit of warmth. Look for neutral colors and flowy, draping silhouettes in soft fabrics.
- **Jeans:** Oh, how I love my jeans—the older and softer, the better. Find a pair that fits your body and style, and then live in them.
- **Neutral flats:** A pair of comfortable, neutral flats are my go-to shoes. I wear them with everything from jeans and shorts to skirts and dresses.
- **Sneakers:** My first choice for days with lots of walking is a pair of simple, white sneakers. Pair them with no-show socks for a fresh spring look.
- **Jewelry:** Whether it's earrings, necklaces, or bracelets, for spring I'm wearing it in the warm metals of gold and copper—nothing too heavy—in classic or vintage styles.
- **Fragrance:** For spring, I prefer a light, floral fragrance with hints of leather and cedar.

SPRING No. 04 TIP

SPRING STEMS

Nothing says, "Hello, spring!" quite like flowers and long stems of leafy greenery. And while I love bringing real blooms into our home, I also decorate with faux stems. They're so ... effortless.

The key is finding faux florals that don't *look* like faux florals. Fortunately, there is an abundance of beautiful and affordable options to choose from. For a more realistic look, avoid anything with unnatural coloring, hard plastic stems, or unnatural textures. Instead, search for pieces with leaves and blooms that vary slightly in color, shape, and size.

For decorating, I'm forever tucking stems of fruit-laden branches and dogwood blooms into vases, vintage glass jars, and painted metal buckets. Gather hydrangea blooms into pots with sprigs of loose, draping greenery. An oversized basket brimming with long, leafy stems and delicate flowers will add light and life to an empty corner. Mingle faux branches

with a few long floral stems and lay them in a wooden trough to create a lovely centerpiece for a table or kitchen island. Or fill a market bag with faux spring stems and hang it on the door or wall for an instant touch of spring.

Faux stems make transitioning from winter to spring so easy and so lovely—and the decorating possibilities are endless.

WHITE COTTAGE FARM

WHERE TO SHOP FOR THE PERFECT FAUX STEMS

Afloral.com			
Target.com			
Bloomist.com			
WorldMarket.com			
ShopTerrain.com			
PotteryBarn.com			
BalsamHill.com			
Amazon.com			

No. 04

see more on
LizMarieBlog.com

a cozy place to share conversation
and comfort food.

SPRING NO. 05 TIP

LAVENDER LATTE

Whether it's coffee, tea, or the occasional soda, I find comfort in always having a beverage by my side, especially when it's reminiscent of the season at hand. Springtime in Michigan offers days of teasing warmth, but there is often still a chill in the air that reminds me it's not quite summer yet. That's why this classic lavender latte is one of my favorite drinks for spring. The subtle taste of lavender calls to mind fresh flower bouquets, while the cozy warmth of the latte is much appreciated on cooler days. Make a cup for yourself, find a relaxing corner, and enjoy a moment of springtime escape.

WHITE COTTAGE FARM

LAVENDER LATTE

Ingredients

- ½ cup hot, strong-brewed coffee (or a shot of espresso, if available)
- 2 tablespoons dried lavender frothed with milk (or, if you prefer something sweeter, add 2 tablespoons lavender syrup, more or less to taste)
- ½ cup milk (I use coconut or almond milk)
- fresh or dried lavender blossoms, optional*

Instructions

1. Add coffee or espresso to your favorite mug and stir in lavender syrup.
2. Heat milk with an espresso machine frother (I like SMEG's espresso machine), or simply heat on the stovetop or in the microwave, and whip with a handheld milk frother.
3. Add milk to coffee.
4. Garnish with fresh lavender blossoms and enjoy!

LAVENDER SYRUP

Ingredients

- 2 cups water
- 1 cup sugar
- 2 tablespoons fresh or dried lavender flowers*

---

*Dried lavender can be found in many cooking stores and online. If using fresh blooms, be sure they are free of pesticides.

Instructions

1. Bring water and sugar to a boil in a small saucepan.
2. Whisk until sugar is dissolved; then remove from heat.
3. Stir in lavender, cover, and steep for about an hour.
4. Strain the syrup and discard the lavender; then cover and store in the refrigerator for up to two weeks.

SPRING BUCKET LIST

The sights, smells, and events of springtime create an irresistible urge to head outside, try something new, and enjoy the simple freshness of the season. Here are a few of my favorite must-dos for spring. Create your own springtime list, and savor every moment!

WHITE COTTAGE FARM

Attend an outdoor flea market.			Play in the rain.	
Visit a flower field.			Look for rainbows.	
Explore a local greenhouse.			Host an Easter brunch.	
Frequent the farmers market.			Have a tea party.	
Head outside for a picnic.			Plant something.	
Have a family day at the zoo.			Go for a bike ride.	
Start a new healthy habit.			Fly a kite on a windy day.	
Create a spring cleaning checklist.			Experiment with a new recipe.	
Do the long-awaited spring chores.			Dye eggs and set up an egg hunt.	
Go for evening walks.			Find a spring-scented candle.	

No. 06

RECEIVED BY

HOW TO USE WHITES IN SPRING

SPRING NO. 07 TIP

Spring décor is my simplest look, because so little is needed to convey the open-air freshness of the season. Whites form the backdrop of it all; they are always a clean and classic choice. I know that many are wary of whites, wondering how something could possibly *stay* white. But our family is living proof that white décor can work— yes, even for those of us with busy toddlers, pets, and all the messy adventures of farm life. The secret is that everything in our home is durable and washable. It does take a bit of work, but ultimately is worth it in the end. (See page 76 for more tips on keeping things white.)

Bring shades of white into your own home in wall colors, in rugs and flooring, and in an assortment of curtains, linens, and throws. Incorporate textures to add dimension and warmth. The art of combining different shades of white is to mix your textures. For example, on a white linen slipcovered sofa, add white wool pillows for a cozy combination of whites. When styling your shelves, cabinets, and vignettes, don't be afraid to mix together your white stoneware, pitchers, vases, and bowls.

Do your whites need to be refreshed? White paint can begin to look a little less fresh and bright over time. Spring is my favorite time to repaint walls, floors, ceilings, and so on to keep paint looking bright if needed. Even if it's already white, you may need a refresh after a few years!

With white as the background, all the colors of spring's palette pop. Layer vibrant greens with the natural wood tones of braided seagrass baskets, natural fiber rugs, and rattan chairs. Their softly muted tones allow the greens to take center stage and encourage the perfection of nature to shine through.

COZY UP YOUR STORAGE

In my world, clutter is inevitable, and spring cleaning is a great time to tackle it. In addition to the everyday clutter of life we all have, I have a huge collection of seasonal pillow covers and inserts, blankets and throws, slipcovers and rugs—even a few pieces of furniture I will never get rid of. Then there are all the décor items, such as stacks of prints, frames, baskets, and stems for every season. And it all needs to be stored. I have a lot of storage in my home that isn't pretty; not all of my storage can or will look pretty. Other spots, like cabinets or shelves, I style to make my storage look cozy.

Doesn't it feel great when you can take the cozy vibe in your home and incorporate it into your storage? It begins with keeping it clean and organized. (So, if there's a closet that's threatening to become an avalanche, take the time to clean it out and organize it. The space—and your mental clutter—will instantly feel cozier.)

COZY UP YOUR STORAGE

For pillows, blankets, and throws, I love storage bags that compress down to a much smaller size, saving precious space. Clear, stackable totes corral seasonal décor and other items, keeping them tucked away while still allowing me a peek inside. To be super-organized (which I occasionally am), add labels so that items are easily located and then just as easily returned once the season has passed.

Go vertical. Think of building shelves vertically and in higher-up spaces for additional storage. We often forget to look up. Baskets on top of the fridge look pretty and are excellent hidden storage! Utilize the tops of cabinets or wardrobes for more storage space. Rework or even redesign your closet systems to better utilize the entire space to suit your individual needs.

Think of ways you can incorporate pretty storage into everyday décor. Baskets and boxes are the perfect way to store your items. I love baskets with lids, which are definitely my go-to for storage out in the open. We use baskets and boxes on shelves, next to the sofa, and on coffee tables for storage.

Though organizing seasonal décor might not seem the most glamorous of decorating challenges, it will give you a lighter feeling just knowing that everything is in its own place, easy to find, and waiting for its time to shine.

WHITE COTTAGE FARM

STORAGE TIPS

Do you have a closet with high ceilings?

Are your beds tall enough for underbed storage?

Do you have a closet you could repurpose for more space?

Could you add cupboards into a laundry room?

Could you clear out space in your basement, garage, or outbuilding?

Is there extra space under your stairs?

Evaluate your space to see what would work best!

No. 08

see more on
LizMarieBlog.com

19

PRIMITIVE WORKBENCH

I love a good DIY, but there's something about making new things in the spring that I particularly enjoy. Is there a piece you've been wanting to add to your home? Furniture in the home doesn't have to be an authentic antique or a vintage treasure to cultivate a cozy vibe. There is another option that is both charming and incredibly versatile: the primitive piece. And when that piece is one you've crafted yourself, it becomes more than just furniture; it becomes a part of your home.

In our mudroom, we have a beautiful primitive workbench. When we found ours, it already had an antique apron sink installed. Yet, even without the sink, this style of workbench is wonderfully functional on its own—for folding laundry, potting flowers, or any activity where a bit more workspace is needed. DIY your own primitive workbench and make it a versatile part of your cozy home.

Make your own simple version out of reclaimed wood to fit a particular space, or if you're feeling like trying your hand at making something a little like ours, visit LizMarieBlog.com for a full set of instructions.

THE ART OF PLANTING A GARDEN

One of my dreams is to have a self-sufficient farm. Although we are far from that goal, each year our garden comes one step closer. Our garden not only helps feed our family but also teaches valuable lessons as we care for and tend to the plants. Nothing is better than being able to provide our friends and family with food from our garden. Not only does gardening help to relax and calm my nerves, it also helps me feel accomplished to see the successful growth each year.

What to grow: For those new to gardening, begin by researching the agricultural zone you live in, as well as the type of soil you have. Take note of which plants will thrive and which will struggle in your area. Next, think about the fruits and vegetables you and your family consume the most, as well as the flowers you love. Give special consideration to those that not only can be enjoyed at harvest time but also can be dried, frozen, or canned for later. Check out local garden clubs—or family and friends—for advice and tips, as well as for sharing seeds and cuttings.

Who Can Grow: We make the most of our gardening spaces. Not only does it leave land available for other uses, but packing everything neatly together cuts down on labor and requires fewer resources, such as water and fertilizer. We want our garden to require minimal effort. Anyone can have a garden, whether it's a few plants in a windowsill, a small backyard garden, or a communal garden.

Sun and Partial-Sun Organization: Once you've decided what you want to grow, consider how much sunlight your chosen seeds, seedlings, and plants will require. Many garden plants need full sun, but there are a few that prefer partial sun. To make the most of your gardening space, pair sun-loving taller plants or trellis plants with those that need partial sun. For example, plant a row of sunflowers, and, after they've grown to a few inches, surround the base of

each with herbs that need partial sun. As the sunflowers grow, they will shade the herbs during the hottest parts of the day.

Root System Staggering: Some plants have deep tap roots, while others have more fibrous roots that grow closer to the surface. Though it may take trial and error to perfect, staggering plants with different root systems will allow you to pack more plants into less space. To begin, take those plants that have deep tap roots and follow the recommended planting distance for them. Then fill in the space between with plants that have more fibrous roots. The tap root plants will access the water and nutrients farther down into the soil, while those with fibrous roots will use the soil nearer the surface.

Grow Up Where Possible: Trellises and arches can greatly increase your yield while having practically no impact on the footprint of your garden. Beans, squash, and gourds easily climb trellises and arches, as do many flowering vines.

Gardening is different for everyone. You may have been born with a green thumb, or perhaps your gardening skills need nurturing. When days are spent in the sunshine, coaxing life from the soil, I find that the harvest is always a joyful one.

COZY TIP: HOW TO USE WHAT YOU GROW IN YOUR GARDEN

Clip flowers throughout the year to display in your home. This is a great way to change up your seasonal décor in centerpieces or vases throughout your home.

Dry or press your florals to display permanently. Make framed art, shadow box art, or even ornaments for your trees.

Start a floral or garden stand to share the treasures of your garden and either trade or make some extra garden spending money.

Give floral arrangements as gifts to loved ones.

Make a wreath with clippings from your yard and garden. Make a mini one for a flower crown!

WHAT TO PLANT IN SPRING

Spring is the time for planting vegetables and flowers as our fingers dig into the soft, rich dirt. Use the early days of the season—when winter's chill has not quite faded—to begin planning and preparing. Consider: Where will beds be tilled? What will be planted and when? Are there seeds that should be started on a windowsill now? Then, when the danger of frost has finally passed, it's time to plant. Here are some of my springtime planting favorites:

WHITE COTTAGE FARM

THE VEGETABLE GARDEN	THE FLOWER GARDEN
Beans	Black-Eyed Susans
Carrots	Clematis
Lettuce	Marigolds
Peas	Purple Coneflower
Radishes	Sunflowers
Zucchini	Zinnias

No. 11

see more on
LizMarieBlog.com

SPRING NO. 12 TIP · COZY EASTER VIGNETTE

Easter evokes for me the beloved scenes of Beatrix Potter and of Peter Rabbit and his button-popping escape from Mr. McGregor's garden. My love for rabbits truly stems from my grandma and her love for Beatrix Potter. This was ingrained in me as a young girl enjoying her displays of Beatrix Potter books, rabbits, and artwork. Over the years I have developed my own collection of vintage rabbit artwork, figurines, and books to match hers.

For this mantel styling, I've chosen a vintage rabbit print as the focal point. I love the touch of whimsy it brings. Antique green glass jars add both light and color, while the wicker basket and faded book provide texture and natural coloring. The finishing touches include an antique pot filled with my favorite greenery. Notice that the elements of each side are not perfectly mirrored but are still nicely balanced.

The simplicity of this look allows it to remain up for all of the spring season, which I love. It gives notes to Easter but can remain up past the holiday, continuing the joy that this rabbit print brings to the vignette.

EVERYDAY COZY

SPRING NO. 13 TIP

When we talk about decorating in a cozy style, we're often discussing how to display collections, use vintage pieces, and incorporate specific elements, such as furniture, linens, accessories, and florals. In other words, it's all about the décor. But a large part of what fills our homes isn't what we would typically consider décor elements. What are we to do with all those necessary, everyday items that make our homes functional?

Make them cozy, of course.

Cozy, to me, has lots of layers, and one of those layers *is* the everyday stuff of life. An important piece of my cozy equation is making sure that all the items in any given space are both useful and loved by me and my family. This especially applies to heavily trafficked areas, like the kitchen, mudroom, and laundry room. Yes, I have décor in these places simply for its visual appeal. But I also adore

finding ways to combine coziness and functionality—particularly in the "working" areas of our home.

So, what if we viewed all the visible items in our homes as décor? And what if we chose even the everyday items of our lives not just for their usefulness but also for their visual potential? Indulge in that coffeepot in a color you love. Rescue wooden spoons from that overflowing drawer and corral them in an old crock. Look for attractive brooms, dusters, and scrub brushes, and hang them from pretty hooks or peg rails. Choose glasses, plates, bowls, and platters that you'll enjoy seeing on your countertop. Dish towels and bath linens needn't be bland to be functional—bring in the colors, patterns, and textures of the season at hand.

When thoughtfully chosen, even the everyday, functional items of our homes become part of the cozy atmosphere.

SPRING–AND SEASONAL– CLEANING

Spring cleaning: it brings to mind thoughts of that yearly deep dive into housework and a giant purge of the things we no longer need, use, or enjoy. But I find that my home feels fresher and more welcoming when I repeat these rituals at the start of every season. The process resets our home, as well as my thoughts for the day and weeks to come. So, use these lists to also inspire your fall, winter, and summer cleaning.

A basic checklist helps you tackle these at your own pace, without feeling rushed or overwhelmed by cleaning the house all at once. Grab your coffee, put on your favorite playlist, and enjoy the process of freshening your home, bit by bit, room by room.

WHITE COTTAGE FARM

QUARTERLY CLEANING AND CHORES

Dust and wipe all surfaces.			Clean out closets.		
Polish furniture.			Change HVAC filters.		
Wash floors and baseboards.			Vacuum refrigerator coils.		
Wipe down walls and touch up paint.			Purge unneeded clothes and toys.		
Clean all knobs and switches.			Organize towels and linens.		
Dust blinds and curtain rods.			Deep clean entire pantry.		
Wash windows and windowsills.			Launder all bedding.		
Dust light fixtures and fans.			Clean under kitchen sink.		
Vacuum upholstered furniture.			Wash shower curtains and liners.		
Clean kitchen cabinet doors and backsplash.			Launder or dry-clean drapes, curtains, and rugs.		
Clean out and organize kitchen drawers.			Clean washer and dryer, including dryer vent.		
Clean and reorganize bathroom storage.			Vacuum and clean vents and registers.		
Wipe down all electronic appliances, following manufacturer's instructions.			Clean all kitchen appliances, inside and out.		
Launder slipcovers, curtains, and throws.			Clean out refrigerator and freezer, defrosting if necessary.		

No. 14

RECEIVED BY

SPRING

NO. 15

TIP

THE ART OF THE VINTAGE VESSEL

It's no secret that I love fresh flowers and greenery. There's such a soul-restoring comfort to be found in tending the garden, in gathering florals from our fields, and in clipping seasonal blooms and branches from our orchards. I suppose it's the desire to re-create that same sense of peaceful, cozy comfort that has me filling our home with flowers, fruit, branches,

stems—anything to surround myself with the beauty of creation.

But all those flowers, branches, and bits of greenery need vessels. My favorites are the antique ones, the ones that seem to tell a story of their own with chipped edges, out-of-the-ordinary colors and textures, and that oh-so-lovely vintage vibe. Over the years, I've collected quite a few from antique fairs, yard sales, and flea markets, as well as from family and friends. It's a collection that I'm forever adding to.

If you are like me, the struggle comes along when we try to style the vessel. Some vintage vessels can't hold water, some are too large to properly hold up stems, and some are not the right shape for styling. My trick to making stems and plants work with the vintage vessel is to put another vessel inside of it. The smaller vessel inside the vintage piece can hold the water, prop up the stems, and prevent any damage to the vintage vessel.

Vintage vessels have enough character to stand on their own as the centerpiece of a cozy vignette. But they serve most beautifully as gathering places for all the lovely blooms and seasonal greens. You can find empty vessels ready and waiting in numerous places in our home—everywhere from the living room to the bathrooms. And I'll confess that having just the right vase or vessel at my fingertips makes me feel so wonderfully grown-up, especially after spending a delightfully childlike afternoon gathering blooms and satisfying that urge to bring the outside in.

WHITE COTTAGE FARM

MY FAVORITE VINTAGE VESSELS

Stoneware pitchers				
Old glass jugs				
Galvanized pails				
Whimsical pots				
Market bags and baskets				
Canning jars				
Enamel pitchers				

No. 15

see more on
LizMarieBlog.com

SPRING

NO. 16

TIP

HANDMADE PLANT MARKERS

With the Midwest's indecisive weather, I must resist the temptation until the last of those few late frosts has melted into memory to put my tender little seedlings in the ground. So I turn to an essential garden DIY that is both deliciously cozy and useful: making plant markers.

I like to include lots of details on my markers. While one side simply includes the plant name, the reverse will often include the planting date, whether it was transplanted from indoor seedlings that I had grown in a pot or directly planted from the nursery, and whether it was planted from purchased seed or seed we harvested ourselves, as well as any other details we might want to remember throughout the growing season. Because we include such detailed information, we usually make new markers each season. But if labeled with only the plant name, markers could be reused each season.

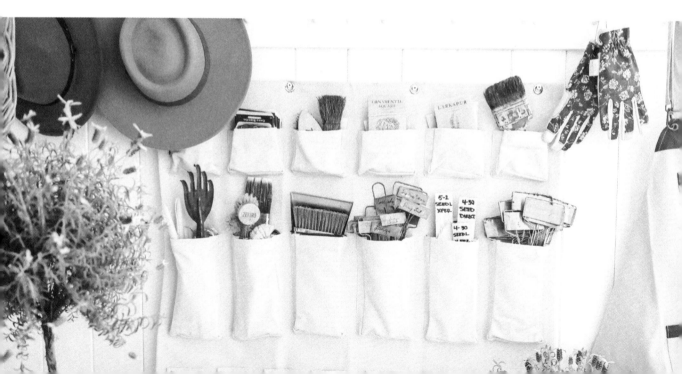

WOOD PLANT MARKERS

Materials:

2 x 4 (or other scrap wood, cut to the dimensions below)

nontoxic paint or stain (optional)

permanent marker

Tools:

table saw

ruler

How To:

1. Using a table saw, rip the wide side of the 2 x 4 wood to a $1/2$-inch thickness.
2. Cut the $1/2$-inch thick wood into strips 6 to 8 inches long. Your pieces will now measure $1/2$ inch x 1 $1/2$ inches x 6 to 8 inches.
3. To make it easier to push the plant marker into the ground, cut corners at the bottom of each strip at a 45-degree angle.
4. To make markers more durable and reusable, coat with a nontoxic, waterproof paint or stain.
5. Use a permanent marker to record any information on the marker.

METAL PLANT MARKERS

Materials:

12 x 12-inch piece of 28-gauge sheet metal

1 bundle of 8-inch outdoor stake flags

Tools:

permanent marker

dremel hand tool with metal-cutting and sanding attachments

carpenter square

needle-nose pliers, with wire-cutter option

clamp

heavy gloves

How To:

1. Use the permanent marker to mark off a grid of 1 x 3-inch rectangles on the sheet metal. These will form the "tag" of your plant marker.
2. Clamp the sheet metal to a sturdy surface. Use the Dremel cutting tool to cut along the grid lines. (Wear heavy gloves to avoid being cut by the metal edges.)
3. Use the Dremel sanding wheel to smooth all the edges.
4. Remove the fabric flags from the outdoor stakes. Bend the legs into a U shape.
5. Take one of the metal rectangles and bend the short edges over each leg of the stake, near the U. Pinch in the corners to keep it from sliding up and down.
6. Use a permanent marker to write your labels.

SPRING NO. 17 TIP

THE VERSATILITY OF SLIPCOVERS

This is my ode to the slipcover. Our home wouldn't be half as cozy without them. Because they are so easy to strip off and wash, slipcovers allow us to actually *live* on our white furniture without worrying about spills, stains, or smudges. And—trust me—in a farmhouse with a toddler, dogs, and the occasional sheep wandering in, dirt is going to happen.

Slipcovers have the added benefit of freshening up a room or changing things up for a season without buying all new furniture. They have been our way of life for years now, and when I purchase an upholstered piece of furniture, I make a custom slipcover for it. From sofas and ottomans to dining room chairs, slipcovers give us that cozy white cottage farmhouse look we love, while also giving us the durability and livability we need.

If you're in the market for furniture with a ready-made slipcover, you have several choices these days. Places like IKEA,

Pottery Barn, Restoration Hardware, and Wayfair offer a variety of well-made options at multiple price points. To find a slipcover for a piece you already have, try IKEA, Bemz.com, or Amazon. For unusual pieces or specific fabrics, custom-made slipcovers are an option. Visit local fabric shops for ideas, patterns, and connections to local seamstresses. Or search on sites such as Facebook Marketplace, craigslist, and Etsy. For super-affordable custom-made slipcovers, use drop cloth as the fabric; it's durable and affordable to purchase.

Be warned, though. Once you've enjoyed the flexibility, durability, and all-around cozy wonderfulness of slipcovers, you won't want to live without them. (For tips on washing and keeping whites white, see page 76.)

BRINGING IN THE LIGHT

Creating an open, airy atmosphere, brimming with warm and natural light, is a key element of the cozy style—yet not all rooms have windows to welcome in that light. While most of our circa-1800s farmhouse was blessed with large windows, when we moved in, there were a few areas that received no natural light. To bring in the light, over the years we've added windows where possible. If you are struggling with dark and windowless rooms, this is one of my top five home renovation recommendations. Yes, it can be a bit costly, but I've found that the results are worth the expense.

However, adding windows isn't always an option. In that case, I've shared some of my favorite ways to bring in the light.

- **Light bulbs:** Use soft white or warm white bulbs to brighten not only the room but also your mood.
- **Lamps and sconces:** Use lamps with sheer shades to bring light down off the ceiling and into the heart of the room. Sconces are perfect for places such as butler's pantries, large closets, basements, interior baths, and long, dark hallways.
- **Cozy glow:** Bring lighting into the space with interesting and unique types of light. Think of things like glow lights in a vase, lights above artwork, wall sconces, and tiny lamps in shelving.
- **Wall and ceiling colors:** Choose paint colors that are light, bright, and fresh—colors with clear, cool undertones, and avoid yellow and orange undertones. Don't forget ceilings and trims; a coat of crisp white paint will instantly brighten the space.
- **Cabinets and furniture:** Cabinets, shelves, countertops, and furniture can bring a lot of darkness into a space. Consider using light paint

colors on cabinets or shelves. Select
countertops with a reflective and
bright finish, such as light quartz.
Choose pieces of furniture with
a light wood tone or light-colored
fabrics.

❦ Reflective surfaces: Accessorize
using reflective surfaces to bounce
that light around and make the
space seem brighter. Think beyond
mirrors to brass, crystal, and glass
accents.

❦ Plants: Plants bring life to dark and
shadowy corners. Try low light–
loving houseplants, such as snake
plant and pothos. Special light bulbs
that double as grow lights will allow
you to bring in other plants. Choose
bulbs that shine with a natural
white light instead of the traditional
pink. Or, if the area is truly dark,
choose high-quality faux plants and
greenery.

❦ Add contrast: Wood tones,
patterned rugs, and artwork add
interest and texture, while also
working to pull the viewer's eye away
from shadowy corners.

FINDING YOUR OWN COZY STYLE

When it comes to the cozy style, there's one thing that is definitely true—and that is that there is *no* one thing that is definitely true. Except perhaps this: your style—cozy or otherwise—should be personal to you.

Creating cozy is what I do. And I am so thrilled and honored when people choose to incorporate my ideas into their homes. Yet I never want anyone to feel that their home must be an exact replica of mine, or that there is only one way to make a home cozy. Instead, I want to encourage you to seek out, cultivate, and nurture your own sense of style. But maybe you're asking, *How on earth do I do that?* Begin with a little thinking, a little searching for inspiration, and a *lot* of dreaming.

Reflect on what you are drawn to. Write down what you love about your spaces already or what you love most about spaces that inspire you. Most people have a stockpile of magazines, books, or digital sources with home décor they love. Compile all of these things to evaluate.

Choose your words or phrases. What words would you use to describe those rooms and homes you love? Is it white, bright, comfortable, or colorful? As you examine your own home and rooms, choose paints, furniture, and accessories that reflect those words. When I think of our home, I tend to think in phrases: *cozy white, authentic antique, updated historic, cottage farmhouse, eclectic collections, French farmhouse.*

Do some thinking. Once you've gathered your collection of ideas, notice what they have in common. Is there a color palette that keeps popping up? Is the style highlighted with vintage or antique accessories? Is there a recurring theme, such as plants and flowers, photographs, or family heirlooms? Do your phrases match your inspiration photos?

Organize your thoughts. Create a file,

notebook, mood board, or a Pinterest page to collect the ideas that catch your eye. I love having the visual of a mood board to work from and to help me make adjustments to see the whole vision.

Do some dreaming. Don't limit yourself to what you see in the photos and homes of others. Dream outside the box. What do you truly want? How could this work better for your family? Is this a trend, or do you love it?

Search for inspiration. Instagram, Pinterest, and other social media sites have given us access to a world of creative and cozy ideas. Dive in and search out homes, styles, and cozy elements that you love.

Review your current space. What items match the style you've defined? What items could you revamp to match your style (a coat of paint, restaining wood, adding new hardware, making a slipcover, replacing pillow covers, etc.)? What items do you need to sell, give away, or donate?

Purchase carefully. Don't feel pressure to buy things simply because they're on sale or because they were featured on someone's post or blog. Collect the things that make your own heart smile.

Tinker and play. Finding your personal cozy style isn't a onetime thing. My own style is constantly growing, changing, and evolving. Don't be afraid to try something and then decide it's not for you. Or try one thing and then move it around. Reimagine. Tinker and play and enjoy the process of creating your own cozy—and personal—style.

Create your home guide. Now that you've reimagined your design style, let's talk about the after. Create a one-page home guide and use it anytime you want to add new items into your home. Does this item match your style? Is it needed in your space? Will it add to or elevate your space? Constantly evaluate what makes you happy in your space and what you love.

CREATE YOUR PERSONALIZED HOME GUIDE

Going out and shopping, choosing finishes, and remembering sizing can be overwhelming. Now that you've found your style, how do you make sure you don't lose it?

I keep a home guide—a list of things I keep with me while out shopping, to help stay on track with my style. Before I had a home guide, I would overbuy because I liked an item without considering whether or not it fit my style. This led to wasting time and money without truly cultivating the home I love. A home guide can help with anything from having measurements with you while at a flea market to having paint colors ready to match with new items.

Keep these in a small notepad, a journal, or an electronic device.

WHITE COTTAGE FARM

FOR EACH ROOM, KEEP A LIST OF THE FOLLOWING

Square footage
Wall and window measurements
Door measurements
Paint colors
Fabrics used
Fixture finish and color
Items you are searching for

No. 20

see more on
LizMarieBlog.com

SPRING NO. 21 TIP

EASTER BASKETS AND EASTER EGGS

Since adopting our son, Cope, I've realized the importance of creating traditions to surround each holiday for our family. My husband, Jose, and I had created traditions around Easter with our extended family, but I love adding new traditions for our little family each year. Cope inspires me to make this holiday, as well as all the reasons behind it, special for us and for him.

That begins, I believe, with traditions. Traditions help us slow down, soak in the meaning of the day, and truly give us and our loved ones a reason to celebrate. So here at the White Cottage Farm, we'll be resurrecting a few of the old, forgotten pastimes as well as creating a few new traditions of our own.

WHITE COTTAGE FARM

COZY EASTER TRADITIONS

Dying Easter eggs with flowers, root vegetables, leaves, and nuts foraged from our farm
Gathering with friends of all ages for an Easter egg hunt
Creating Easter baskets for the whole family (even our dogs, Winnie, Bear, and Bella)
Dressing in our Sunday best and taking a family photo to remember the day
Playing outside and teaching Cope all the old-fashioned games of our childhoods
Visiting with family, near and far
Explaining to Cope the importance of Easter Day
Worshiping together as a family

No. 21

see more on
LizMarieBlog.com

COZY TIP: PERSONALIZED BASKETS

I love the idea of each family member having a personalized basket to use year after year. To create your own, simply purchase a basket and wooden letters to spell out each name. Hot glue the letters to the basket, painting them first, if you like. Then fill the basket to the brim. For Cope, I like to include books and a stuffed bunny, lamb, or deer, along with an heirloom-worthy wooden toy or two. Our book *We Belong to Each Other* makes an excellent addition to any child's Easter basket!

A MOTHER'S DAY CELEBRATION

Here at the farm, Mother's Day includes *all* the moms. I take time away from everyday responsibilities to appreciate and celebrate these special ladies—the moms, the grandmas, Cope's birth mom, my neighbor Diane, and all the other "grandmas" we have adopted into our lives.

To show appreciation for the moms and mom figures in our lives, I love to do something special just for them. Though the specifics vary from year to year, I love gifting in ways that delight our five senses. Think of gifts that may appeal to sight, smell, sound, touch, and taste. All are shared around a brunch or dinner, where tempting treats mingle with the sounds of laughter and conversation. It's a time for lingering, for reminiscing, and for sharing all those timeless, tried-and-true tips we new mothers so long to hear. For me, it's a time for holding Cope close as I celebrate my membership in this tribe of amazing women.

Sometimes the thought of entertaining feels overwhelming. However, these lovely ladies in our lives deserve to be celebrated, and brunch is my favorite way to do it. Depending on where you live, you can host indoors, outdoors, or even at a local park! For Mother's Day I love to turn this into a garden-inspired event. The key here is flowers. Create simple centerpieces or mini bouquets with fresh or faux stems. Garnish dishes, beverages, and desserts with flower petals or herbs, or with fresh berries and citrus. Dress this event up or down to your liking, as it will be a crowd-pleaser either way.

You can invite the whole family to celebrate these special ladies in your life or make it a "ladies only" gathering. Either way, focusing on the people we love and the gift of motherhood is what makes it most worth celebrating.

WHITE COTTAGE FARM

MOTHER'S DAY GIFT IDEAS

Hanging plant baskets	
Book or cookbook you love	
Piece of memorable jewelry	
Utilitarian item that will bring her joy	
Her classic beauty favorites	
Throughout the year, jot down things she mentions but won't buy for herself.	

No. 22

see more on
LizMarieBlog.com

SUMMER

SUMMER

Summer. It calls to mind images of rocking chairs on the front porch as evening falls, the soft whir of a fan, and the smell of freshly mown grass layered with the scents of blooming flowers. While the soaring temperature sends many hurrying inside to air-conditioned comfort, I find the opposite to be true for our family. Summer is the season we live outside, tending to gardens, to sheep, and to bees. These are the days we spend as much time as possible splashing in the pool, floating at the lake, and relaxing on a picnic blanket. It's the season of blooms and barbecues, of fresh-squeezed lemonade and the Fourth of July. It's the crackling of sparklers and teaching Cope to catch fireflies as we run barefoot and giggling on those long summer days. Summer is the season that warms my skin and nurtures my soul.

When we do step inside, I bring much of that outdoor life along with me. I find myself lingering in the garden in my favorite floppy hat, gardening shears in hand, and filling my arms with blooms to fill antique vases, old metal buckets, vintage baskets, and market bags. And all those wonderful vegetables we planted in spring are just beginning to ripen and fill our table. These are the days of refreshing and rearranging our décor and tackling DIYs. The inside of our home replicates the light and breezy feeling of summer, which is summer cozy to me.

SUMMER DÉCOR STAPLES

SUMMER
NO.
23
TIP

Fresh, clean, and *bright*—these are the words that inspire my summertime décor. My summer is spent browsing flea markets and collecting goodies to honor the era our home originated in and bringing it back to the eclectic antique farmhouse it is meant to be. I'm basically a squirrel gathering nuts for the winter—exploring flea markets and antique shops to store up goods for future months.

Though some might say cozy is better suited to cooler days, I have to disagree. Cozy for me is all about creating an atmosphere, a sense of welcome that says, "Come in, and be comfortable here with us all year round." And while there are a million different ways to incorporate coziness into your home, here are a few of the staples I find myself using each year as summer approaches.

Pots and planters: Containers—when filled with greenery and blooms—add texture, life, and light to a room. Aged clay pots, silver urns, and stoneware pitchers are always beautiful. Look for unique pots and planters online, or repurpose vintage finds, such as a small old stoneware crock spilling over with pothos.

Blooms: Summer is the season of flowers. Cut them from your own garden, purchase them from a local greenhouse, or pick them up during your trip to the grocery store. For season-long color, invest in worry-free faux stems.

Linens, pillows, and throws: Though the heat of the season might seem to exclude these layers, there's something cozy about curling up with a light linen sheet or thin cotton throw under the icy blast of air-conditioning. And lounging on a pile of freshly slipcovered pillows for an afternoon nap—what could be more refreshing?

Mirrors and reflective surfaces: Include them in vignettes to lend a light and airy feel. Think beyond mirrors to cool silvers and bright brasses in the form of platters, vases, planters, and wall hangings.

Nature-inspired items: Whether you like the beach or florals, bring items inspired by that into your décor. Think of driftwood centerpieces, watercolored throws, floral-printed tea towels, and artwork that brings in nature or embodies the feeling of summertime.

NO.
24

SUMMER

TIP

SUMMER WARDROBE STAPLES

For me, summertime is all about soaking up the outdoors, so I'm looking for clothes that will keep me cool while still being cozily cute and stylish. Michigan temps might not soar as high as in other parts of the country, but soft, breezy, breathable fabrics are still very much appreciated. While I don't consider myself a fashionista, I do love to bring cozy into all facets of my life. And if you're wondering how to create a cozy wardrobe in summer's heat, remember that touches of white always create a cool-yet-cozy feel. Here are a few of my summertime favorites:

Cotton Tees: Oh-so-soft and oh-so-essential, cotton tees are a staple in my wardrobe. I love them in neutral, go-with-everything shades of charcoal, light gray, and—of course—shades of white. These are great for layering under fun pieces like kimonos, light cardigans, or jean jackets.

Shorts: I love shorts—the staple of summertime—in natural, breathable fabrics and styles that move with me as I chase Cope around the farm. I find that white, chambray, and linen go with just about anything.

Skirts: Long, soft, and flowy—and often floral—skirts are a go-to in summer. So cool and easy to slip on, pair them with a crisp white blouse or tee to feel instantly put together.

Sandals and Slip-Ons: Quick and cool is the name of the game for summertime footwear. Sandals are perfect for dressier moments or for simply dressing up jeans. And I've discovered that low or no heels are much easier for chasing after little boys bent on adventure. Canvas slip-ons pair effortlessly with shorts and jeans—and make slipping outside at a moment's notice a breeze.

Swimsuits and Cover-Ups: Whether you're lounging at the lake, on the beach, or by a backyard pool, summer days call for swimwear. With Cope to watch over, I look for suits that let me move without worry and cover-ups that let me shift easily from indoors to outdoors.

Sunglasses: Sunglasses are the ultimate accessory for the sunshiny months. Look for shades with UVA/UVB protection. Polarized lenses are a plus. Choose a shape and color to match your own personal style. For me, I love the tortoiseshell color in a slightly retro cat's-eye frame.

Hair Ties and Claw Clips: If you have longer hair, ties are a must to keep hair up and out of the way. I like ones with a bit of personality. A soft, drooping bow in a leopard print or solid neutral is always a winner. If you have shorter hair, claw clips are perfect to quickly secure your hair, and they come in all kinds of colors.

Floppy Hats: For gardening, for sunbathing, for all the days spent outdoors, a floppy hat is a must. My favorites are made of seagrass. They block the sun, make you look instantly put together, and are perfect for those days when your hair just won't cooperate.

Fragrance: For me, summer calls for fragrances that are light, crisp, and fresh. If you like florals, this is the perfect time to bring out the rose, lavender, and jasmine. Choose a lighter scent that is subtle yet fresh. I love the Barr-Co. Original Scent Eau de Parfum, a classic, light, crisp scent.

SUMMER STEMS

Summer is the season of flowers. Their colors make me want to fill my arms with blooms and bring them all inside. Real or faux, summer stems add life and warmth to your cozy décor. When bringing stems inside, be sure to prune them and change the water often. Add a splash of soda or bleach to the water to keep your stems looking beautiful longer. Though stems grow best with sunlight outside, when you bring them indoors, keep them out of direct light, excess heat, and away from fruits.

For lasting arrangements, faux stems offer a wide variety of options. Use them to add pops of worry-free, low-maintenance color. For information on what to look for and where to shop, see page 10.

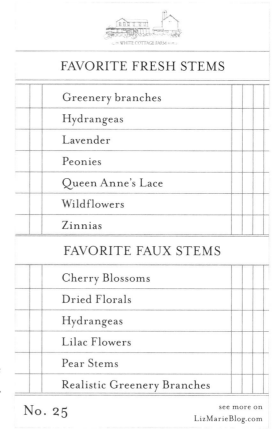

WHITE COTTAGE FARM

FAVORITE FRESH STEMS

Greenery branches	
Hydrangeas	
Lavender	
Peonies	
Queen Anne's Lace	
Wildflowers	
Zinnias	

FAVORITE FAUX STEMS

Cherry Blossoms	
Dried Florals	
Hydrangeas	
Lilac Flowers	
Pear Stems	
Realistic Greenery Branches	

No. 25

see more on
LizMarieBlog.com

COZY TIP: HOW TO KEEP YOUR STEMS FRESH LONGER

1. Bring a bucket of water with you when picking stems so there is no drying time.
2. Run under warm water and trim the ends of your stems before putting into a vase.
3. Add flower preservative to the water or make your own plant food.

SUMMER
NO.
26
TIP

FRESH LEMONADE

Summertime is made for freshly squeezed lemonade—or perhaps lemonade is freshly made for summertime. And though we often think of it as a drink for the kids, it's a cozy summer staple here on the farm, making it my go-to drink for guests of all ages. Served in a sparkling glass pitcher, fresh lemonade not only offers a refreshing retreat from summer's hot sun but also creates a beautiful centerpiece as friends gather round. Mix up your own ice-cold pitcher, and sip the afternoon away.

RECIPE

Makes approximately 1/2 gallon of lemonade.

Ingredients

- 2 cups sugar
- 2 cups water
- 2 cups fresh-squeezed lemon juice (8 to 10 lemons)
- 4 to 6 cups cold water
- Lemon slices, fresh berries, mint sprigs, for garnish (optional)

Instructions

1. Begin by making a simple syrup: Stir together sugar and 2 cups of water in a saucepan.
2. Heat to a simmer and continue stirring until sugar is completely dissolved.
3. Remove from heat and allow to cool.
4. Squeeze the juice from lemons to get 2 cups of juice.
5. Stir simple syrup and lemon juice together in a serving pitcher. Add 4 to 6 cups of cold water, to taste. Serve chilled.
6. Garnish with lemon slices. Or add your own flavorful touch with freshly cut slices of strawberries, juicy raspberries, mint sprigs, or a hint of lavender syrup (see page 13).

SUMMER S'MORES

In summer, we love having a fire in the firepit. It's the perfect way to finish off the day, perhaps enjoying a late dinner together as a family or sharing laughter and conversation with a few friends. The firepit anchors the outdoor space and gives us a cozy place to gather.

And when it comes to entertaining, nothing could be easier than gathering around that crackling fire on a star-filled night and indulging in this classic summertime treat. There's no planning, no fancy meal to fuss over, no decorations to worry about. A few logs on the fire and a circle of cozy chairs create the most welcoming space. Simply gather a handful of fire skewers for roasting the marshmallows and pull over a small table to hold platters loaded with marshmallows, graham crackers, and chocolate bars. Get

creative with dark chocolates, peanut butter cups, caramels, coconut, or bits of candied bacon. Or keep it deliciously simple with the tried-and-true traditional treats.

We're always prepared with a stack of wood ready to burn and the ingredients for s'mores on hand, so impromptu gatherings with those we love are effortless. I find that it's these simple outdoor activities, shared with those who matter most, that create the coziest of memories.

Sometimes the coziest thing is simply doing these outdoor activities with friends and family, rather than always focusing on making the prettiest little spaces. I want to emphasize that the fun and cozy memories are the ones you make, and it's not necessary to overthink and overplan every space or event to the smallest details. Enjoying the time with others and what you have created is always more important than how the design turned out.

COZY PICNIC

Whether you embrace the traditional blanket and basket or go all out with crystal, china, and tablecloths, picnics are a ritual of summertime. And the coziest of picnics are the ones you create yourself and share with those you love.

I like to keep a blanket tucked inside a market bag, along with a few picnic

essentials, so we're always ready to head outside. Jose and I have found that Saturdays, random Tuesdays, or pretty much any sunny day offers the perfect excuse to escape to the outdoors for a picnic and playtime with Cope. We don't worry about planning the food, but instead grab whatever is in the fridge or place a quick to-go order from one of our favorite restaurants. Our most memorable picnics are the spur-of-the-moment dinners or lunches out with the sheep or just outside the garden.

Other times picnics provide the opportunity to get a bit more creative—perhaps when friends and family are invited, or when it's a romantic outing just for Jose and me. These are the times I bring out the tables and tablecloths. It might be a casual, low table of planks balanced on bricks or blocks of wood. Or it might be a formal table and chairs. Or I might simply throw out a blanket and pile on plush pillows for lounging.

When time allows for a bit of extra effort, I love the contrast of crystal and china paired with the rustic hues of nature. And with the grass and trees as the backdrop, décor is effortless. If you have a yard or nearby fields and forests, gather branches and blooms to fill the table. Tuck into vases, ceramic pots, wicker baskets, or metal pails—or simply lay them along the table for an oh-so-easy yet elegant touch. Whether you

have a tiny outdoor space or acres to roam, an outdoor table, some sparkly string lights, and an evening of al fresco dining will fill you and your loves with cozy summertime memories.

On these more planned and formal occasions, I like to go beyond traditional picnic fare. Platters of fruit and wedges of cheese, a caprese salad, garlic bread slathered with butter—choose foods that delight not only the sense of taste but also of sight

and scent as well. A wheeled garden cart is perfect for holding an array of beverages.

As with all things cozy, the focus is not on perfection, but rather on making everyone feel welcomed, thought of, and well taken care of. Whether it's in the park, the meadow, or the backyard, a picnic is a wonderful way to pause and inject a bit of extraordinary into the ordinary days of life. After all, the coziest picnic is the one you actually go on.

CAMPING COZY STYLE

There's something so appealing about getting back to the solid reality of nature. But "roughing it" on a traditional camping trip isn't for everyone. Perhaps that's why *glamping*—glamorous camping—has become so popular in recent years. Though it might sound a bit intimidating and tough to pull off, to me glamping is simply a way to make spending time outdoors as cozy and comfortable as possible. Whether you have a fully decked-out RV with all the comforts of home or a cozy tent with twinkle lights and piles of pillows, the glamping options are as endless as they are individual.

Camping can be as luxurious as our hearts desire and our budgets allow, but there are also lots of affordable options. Consider renting an RV or even an Airstream and reserve a spot in a park across town or across the nation. Invest in a tent and explore your local campgrounds, or a friend's meadow, or even your own backyard.

WHITE COTTAGE FARM

ADD THESE EXTRAS FOR A COZY CAMPOUT

Comfortable outdoor seating
Picnic blankets and piles of pillows for lounging
Light throws for cooler evenings
Portable lighting and lanterns, along with a power source
Favorite foods, snacks, and beverages
Campfire and s'more supplies
Portable projector for a movie night
Outdoor rug to expand your living space
Foldable table for dining

No. 29

see more on
LizMarieBlog.com

64

SUMMER BUCKET LIST

For our family, summer's heat means splashing in the cool waters of lakes and swimming pools, snacking on popsicles, and soaking up the sunshine. Here are just a few of my favorite summer must-dos. What's on your list?

WHITE COTTAGE FARM

SUMMER BUCKET LIST

Camp in the backyard.			Visit the library.		
Feed the ducks.			Watch a fireworks show.		
Take in a baseball game.			Read a book outside.		
Spend a ton of time in the garden.			Visit a county fair.		
Go fishing.			Make popsicles.		
Build a bonfire and make s'mores.			Spend the day at the zoo.		
Host a barbecue.			Shop at a farmers market.		
Take a trip to the beach.			Catch fireflies.		
Gather wildflowers and make a bouquet.			Dance in the rain or run through the sprinklers.		
Jump in a lake, or tube down a lazy river.			Center recipes around what's growing in the garden.		
Grab a blanket and head outside to gaze up at the stars.			Doze in a hammock or nap by a pool.		

No. 30

RECEIVED BY

SUMMER
NO.
31
TIP

GARDEN FENCING

Few things say "cozy cottage charm" quite like a garden wrapped in white picket fencing. At White Cottage Farm, when we want to enclose a garden area, add a decorative border, or just need a bit of light-duty fencing, we like to keep it simple by using premade PVC fencing. It's made of durable vinyl and comes in individual panels, making it so easy to customize to fit the needs of your space. Fencing panels are available in a variety of styles and can be picked up at local hardware or big-box stores, or they can be ordered online.

Begin by choosing the space you want to enclose and measure all around. After purchasing the needed fencing, follow the product instructions to assemble and install. It's that easy.

Jose and I used these premade panels to fence in the garden area near our greenhouse, and we couldn't be happier with the results. Not only is it effective in keeping wildlife out of our vegetables, it gives the space definition, security, and beauty all at the same time.

Could we have built something ourselves? Absolutely. But we gave ourselves permission to not make this one from scratch, freeing up our time and resources for other projects—because cozy doesn't have to be complicated.

Think outside the box for fencing, whether it goes around your garden, around bushes at the front of your house, or alongside your yard. On our travels we fell in love with the creative ways other countries used fencing. I dream to one day have live privacy fencing surrounding the front of our house—not only will it be beautiful to look at, but it will also give us much-needed privacy.

COZY GETAWAY SPOT

I believe everyone—children included—needs a space to call their own. Somewhere to slip away to when they need to remember who they are apart from all the to-dos. Please don't misunderstand—I love all the busyness of my farm. But sometimes I need to put all that aside and just be Liz for a moment. I need a space where I can create and dream and plan.

Not everyone is able to transform an entire room, so if that isn't currently an option, think about where you could tuck a desk or space for creating. Is there a cozy couch and chair for dreaming? Maybe a coffee bar to sip your morning coffee? A hammock or a swing? It doesn't need to be a large space; it just needs to be a spot for you to unwind and focus on what matters most to *you*.

Whether it's a detached she shed or simply a spot in the home, I believe everyone can carve out a cozy space for themselves somewhere—and we all deserve a place that encourages and enhances our me-time. We are the best versions of ourselves when we can spend time cultivating and nourishing our needs.

COZY TIP: CREATING SPACES WITH PURPOSE

My number-one tip would be to make sure you create a space that fulfills a meaningful purpose for you—and is not just another thing to take care of and clean. So think about how you would use a she shed or other space. Do you . . .

- paint or craft? A sunny she shed could be a wonderful studio.
- love gardening? Consider a small greenhouse for your space.
- need a home office? Go for a room or corner in your home with minor changes.
- want to read, nap, rest, or have a place to invite your girlfriends over? Go for the she shed or consider what you can do with a back porch space.

FRESH AND COZY
GUEST ROOMS

We love hosting friends and family at the farmhouse, and we frequently entertain. But because many of our loved ones live nearby, overnight guests are something of a rarity. While we want to have a place to welcome such guests, we are reluctant to dedicate an entire room just for those occasional visits.

We found the solution to our dilemma in an oversized sleeper sofa. This space also functions as our back living room and play area for Cope. When we have guests over, we move the coffee table aside to function as a nightstand when the bed is needed. On a daily basis the coffee table makes a perfect spot for Cope to color, play, or read books!

If space is tight or overnight guests are rare, consider which areas in your home can be multipurposed. Might an office do double duty as a guest room? Even a family room sofa can be made cozy with piles of pillows and a soft blanket or coverlet. Not everyone can convert an entire sofa into a guest bed, but think of other things that may work—like air mattresses, portable cots, or thick throw beds that you can unroll when needed. The simple truth is this: making guests feel comfortable is not so much about the furniture or the space as it is about the thoughtful welcome and little touches.

COZY TIPS FOR WELCOMING GUESTS

Prepare the guest area ahead of time.

Have throw blankets and pillows readily available for guest comfort.

Fill a basket with those oft-forgotten essentials.

Place a table nearby for a glass of water, reading glasses, a lamp, and a bedside book.

Share Wi-Fi passwords and other important or helpful information.

Plan for meals, and make snacks and drinks readily available.

Provide a closet, a drawer, or a special space for guests to put their things.

Implement items that make you feel comfortable when you are away from home.

No. 33

see more on
LizMarieBlog.com

COZY CEILINGS

When we talk about making our homes cozy—regardless of the season, space, or style—there's one area we often neglect: the ceilings. Yet they are the largest, most exposed, and least obstructed surfaces in our homes. Our floors are usually covered with rugs, tables, sofas, and other furniture pieces. Similarly, walls are broken up with windows, gallery walls, and cabinetry. But ceilings—apart from lighting, perhaps—are largely a blank canvas. Why not use that canvas to make a space even cozier?

Some of my favorite homes have exposed floor joists. I love this design element for so many reasons, from the lines of the joists that pull your eyes across the room to the exposed flooring between each joist.

At a minimum, I recommend painting ceilings every five to ten years to keep them looking bright and clean. I've found that while a fresh coat of paint will do wonders for our walls, if the ceiling is yellowed, stained, or out-of-date, the fullness of the effect will be lost. To create a cozy ceiling, there are several options.

- The simplest option is to paint the ceiling with a fresh, clean, and bright white. I prefer to use a matte or ultra-matte white paint because the white already adds reflective quality, so I don't need the additional reflective quality of high-gloss paint.
- Another option is to bring the wall color up onto the ceiling to give the room that "jewel box" effect. This can work even with the boldest of colors. Don't be afraid to experiment. If it doesn't work for the space, simply paint over it.
- Older homes are often dated by their popcorn ceilings. Scrape or sand off all the texture and freshen with a coat of paint.
- For something a bit more involved, install bead board or shiplap on the ceiling for a truly authentic, cozy cottage style.
- Or tear out the ceiling to expose floor joist beams or create your own faux beams (see more on LizMarieblog.com about these options).

KEEPING WHITES WHITE

Clearly, I love white, and this tip is my ode to white. It is the freshest, crispest, coziest color of them all! If you know me at all, you know my love for white décor runs deep. From bed linens and T-shirts to tea towels and slipcovers, layers of white in my home bring me a sense of peace and calm that I can't explain.

Yes, I know white interiors can be intimidating. But after living at White Cottage Farm for a few years now, with its many animals, people, and big, active farm life going on, I can tell you that using white in your home is possible with the proper maintenance. Whether it's keeping new whites as crisp as the day you brought them home or restoring antique whites to their original brightness, here are some of my best laundering tips.

Quick disclaimer: always consider the type of fabric you are using and whether or not these methods will work for that specific fabric.

Grab the baking soda: Let me just say that adding baking soda to every load of laundry is never a bad idea. It's a simple step that boosts your detergent's cleaning power and really works to get the grime out of your whites.

Slice up some lemons: Lemons are packed with acidic power, making them a best friend for your white fabrics. Add a cup of lemon juice to your wash and see how it attacks stains with its natural cleansing ability. Got a tough, smelly stain? Simply cut up a lemon and place it in a pot with enough water to cover the soiled item (but don't add the item yet!). Bring to a boil and then remove from the heat. Place your stained item in the pot and soak overnight.

Pour in the peroxide: Hydrogen peroxide is wonderful for removing those dingy yellow stains from your whites. Add one cup to your washer's bleach dispenser or to your warm water wash, and soak. I try to do this every other wash to keep my whites bright.

Use an oxygen bleach alternative: I love traditional bleach, but the oxygen alternative is gentler on fabrics and often more effective. A bonus is that it can be used to remove stains on colored fabrics as well.

Pull out the vinegar: Soak your whites in white vinegar for an added cleaning punch when washing them. I love doing this with our curtains, bedding, and slipcovers. For oversized pieces, I place them in a bathtub full of hot water, along with one-half cup distilled white vinegar, and let them soak for a few hours or overnight.

Hang them out to dry: The sun's ultraviolet rays are the most affordable and natural way to whiten whites and disinfect fabrics for the freshest-smelling linens. I also love that I don't have to worry about fabrics shrinking or run the dryer all day to keep up with the laundry. Note: If you do use the dryer, be sure to set it on low heat and remove your items while they are still damp so you don't singe fabrics or shrink your slipcovers.

COZY TIP: HOW TO KEEP WHITE LAUNDRY WHITE

- Skip the fabric softener, as it can add a dingy residue to white fabrics.
- Soften hard water with Borax.
- Add liquid dish soap to whiten whites. (It's not just for your dishes!)
- Use the correct amount of laundry detergent and bleach. Overdoing the soap can gray your whites.
- Use optical brighteners or bluing agents. These add a tint of blue, canceling out the yellow in your whites.

SEASONLESS DÉCOR

Few things bring me more joy than making our home cozy throughout all the different holidays and seasons. But decorating for the seasons can be overwhelming—from finding just the right accent items to the actual act of decorating and then figuring out how to store all those seasonal pieces. Storage especially can quickly become an issue. But what if we didn't have to store quite so much? What are those basic décor items we can use throughout the year? Sounds too good to be true, right? But with a few strategic choices in what we purchase, it's completely possible. Here's how:

Baskets and crocks: Woven baskets and crocks in creams and whites are the perfect gathering places for seasonal stems and greenery. Neutral colors and tones allow you to use the same pieces throughout the year.

Framed pictures and prints: "Seasonless" prints and pictures of loved ones can be used as key elements in any season's décor.

Furniture: Furniture pieces provide a place to display any season's vignettes and decorations. Choose cabinets and tables with doors and drawers to tuck linens or other, more seasonally specific items inside.

Pillows: Invest in the comfiest, coziest pillow inserts for couches, benches, and chairs. Pair with seasonal pillow covers, which are so easy to swap out and store away in a drawer.

Faux greenery: Choose greenery and stems that can quickly be transitioned from one season to the next with the addition of a few touches. Look for stems and greenery without literal seasonal touches and instead opt for simple plants and stems.

Utilitarian items: When it comes to my everyday essentials, I like to find the prettiest versions of these items and keep them out all year mixed in with our other décor. This includes brooms, dustpans, scissors, pitchers, measuring cups, and more.

Jars and dishes: We have a lot of different places in our home where we like to use jars, from the kitchen to bookshelves. I always search for jars in a neutral color palette to complement my seasonal items. Dishes are a great décor item in the kitchen. I particularly love white vintage stoneware, as it can stay out all year.

Hooks and peg rails: Use hooks and peg rails as the base for styling décor through every season, and simply switch out the items displayed on them as needed.

HOW TO PAINT FURNITURE

Painting furniture is a great way to repurpose and reuse pieces you already have. It can also bring new life and cozy charm to garage sale and flea market finds. If you've never painted furniture before, it can be a bit intimidating. But I promise it is fun—and often addicting! Here are some of my best tips and tricks for painting furniture:

THE RIGHT PAINT

Every successful project starts with the right paint. Many of the bigger brands—like Behr, Sherwin-Williams, and Benjamin Moore—have paints specifically made for painting furniture and cabinets, which are great options. If you have home décor shops or boutiques in your area, check to see if they carry milk paint or mineral paint. Milk paint usually comes in an easily mixed powder. It will typically leave a subtle crackle in the finish, which fits beautifully with older furniture pieces. My favorite paint by far, though, is mineral paint. It has great coverage and durability, and in most cases, sanding before painting becomes optional.

TO SAND OR NOT TO SAND

Because I most often use mineral paint, I rarely sand my furniture projects. I do clean them before painting, however, using a lint-free cloth and cleaner. I typically use Simple Green cleaner to clean my furniture before painting, though there are several options out there, as many paint companies create their own cleaners. So, when should you sand? If there are rough spots that you want smoothed away, or if you want to ensure a smooth final finish, you'll want to sand. Choose a medium-grit sandpaper, and move with the grain. Be sure to follow up with tack cloth to remove any residue before painting.

APPLYING THE PAINT

If you are painting raw wood, or if you can see the direction of the wood grain of an already painted piece, use a brush to apply the paint in the direction of the grain. If you cannot see the grain, apply the paint in the direction of the longest edge. Because I like a bit of texture on the finished piece, I do not always sand between coats. But it you want a super-smooth finish, sand between coats with a fine-grit sandpaper, being sure the paint is completely dry first.

SEALING THE PAINT

Most paint brands sell sealers that go along with their paint. The decision, then, is what sheen you would like your piece to have. High-gloss sealers leave your piece with a very shiny finish, while eggshell sealers have only a faintly shiny finish. For furniture, I recommend the matte or flat finish, which gives furniture a warmer, cozier vibe. You can also use a wax or polyurethane sealer for your furniture. I like wax for furniture that won't be used every day or spilled on. I recommend polyurethane for any surface you will be eating or cooking at, which makes it easier to wash and more durable for everyday use. Polyurethane comes in finishes in everything from matte to high-gloss.

COZY TIP: FAVORITE FURNITURE PAINTS

- My go-to white furniture paint is Raw Silk Fusion Mineral Paint (see pages 81 and 82).
- Our painted doors are Putty Fusion Mineral Paint.
- Our coffee table is Bedford Fusion Mineral Paint.
- For painting cabinets, I use Benjamin Moore Cabinet Paint.

NO.
38

HOW TO BLEACH FURNITURE

Bleach and *furniture* might not seem like two words that readily go together. But when wood bleach is used on wood furniture, the results are cozy, rustic, raw wood perfection. When you have a beautifully structured wood piece, but the finish is just too dark, give bleaching a try. It can remove stains and lighten the overall tone. Be sure to tackle this project outside—it can get messy!

WHITE COTTAGE FARM

Materials:

wood furniture piece to be
    bleached
wood bleach

Tools:

small scrub brush
coarser scrub brush
bucket for mixing
dry cloth
bucket and hose for rinsing

How to:

1. Mix wood bleach in a bucket according to package directions.
2. Apply mixture to the wood using a small scrub brush, coating the wood heavily. Be sure to brush with the grain and not against it.
3. Next, use a coarser scrub brush to really strip the wood.
4. Depending on how stained your piece is, apply multiple coats. Allow the wood to dry between each coat of bleach.
5. After applying the final coat, allow it to dry fully, then rinse off the piece with water and dry it with a clean cloth.
6. Place the wooden piece in the sunshine to dry fully.
7. Coat with a sealer, if desired.

A PERFECT FATHER'S DAY GIFT

It's easy to forget the men of the family when styling our homes. Some men are super involved in home décor and the decorating process, and for others, it just isn't their thing. But carving out a space for them is just as essential as carving out a space for yourself. Whether this is a spare room in the house, converting the garage space, rearranging your basement area, putting a shed or workshop in the backyard, or finding the perfect chair in your living room—it's important that everyone in the family has their own space that they love.

Jose loves to do woodwork, and I wanted to create a man cave of sorts for him, for his passions and hobbies. Our shed has served many different purposes, and for Father's Day, I transitioned it into a woodworking shop for Jose. The shed now stores all of his tools, woodworking items, and other hobby essentials. The men in your life may have different hobbies or interests, but it is equally important to find a space for them to enjoy and pursue these passions.

One year, we chose to create this as Jose's Father's Day gift, but not all Father's Day gifts are going to be that extravagant. There are so many ways to show appreciation for the father figures in your life, and the way to do so will change based on their interests and hobbies. Any father figure appreciates the big and small gestures; it truly is the thought and moments spent together that mean the most!

CREATING COZY WITH COLLECTED FABRICS

So much of living cozy involves fabrics. It's the feel of a soft cotton throw. It's the splash of a colorful table runner against a white tablecloth. It's the light linen fabric draped over the sofa. Oh, the fabrics! From throws and pillow covers to tablecloths and runners, I love all the fabrics. But buying new linens and fabrics whenever I want to do a refresh around the farmhouse can quickly get expensive. My solution? Collect *all* the fabric!

I scour antique shops for vintage tablecloths, bedspreads, and even remnants, which can often be purchased inexpensively. Clearance racks of department stores and big-box stores can yield a treasure trove of patterned sheets. If you ever want to find me at Pottery Barn, head straight to the clearance section; I'll be digging through baskets for all the cozy white linens. And I'm not above begging for those unused pieces from my grandmother's linen closet.

These stashes of fabric can be useful for all kinds of DIY projects. Bunch up fabric along the center of the dining

or kitchen table for a table runner. Swirl around pots and under trees to camouflage a less-than-attractive container. Drape over a sofa for an impromptu slipcover. Lay your linens across the foot of the bed to add color and pattern to a space. For each season, the most affordable way to add a new pop of color to your bedroom is adding fabric acting as a throw blanket. Or tear into strips and tie onto a length of twine to create a rustic ribbon garland. Fabric offers endless opportunities for creating cozy, so collect all the beautiful fabrics—you never know when or where you might need it.

COZY TIP: REIMAGINE WAYS TO USE YOUR FABRIC

- Turn into pillowcases.
- Use as curtains.
- Drape over tables as tablecloths.
- Lay over furniture for a makeshift slipcover.
- Turn into dish towels.
- Repurpose as gift wrap.
- Sew into reusable pouches and bags.
- Create DIY sachets for a natural room freshener.

SUMMER
NO.
41
TIP

DISPLAYING FAMILY PHOTOGRAPHS

Do you have a favorite cozy memory from your childhood? One of my most treasured memories is of a night when I was only three years old. I sat with my mom out on our screened-in porch and watched as a thunderstorm rolled in. The rain pattered down and the thunder beat out a drumroll as lightning lit up the sky, but I was safe and warm in my mom's arms. I also remember countless family trips to cabins up north, where days were filled with jumping off docks, boat rides on the lake, and deep belly

laughs, while evenings brought bonfires and nighttime adventures.

If you're like me, your most precious memories are the ones filled with family and loved ones. I want to be surrounded by the people who matter most to me. Photographs allow me to bring loved ones, faraway family, and sweet memories into our home. I even incorporate photos of family from the long-ago past—people we've never met—because who they were is part of who we have become.

I don't display family photos all over our home, but I am intentional about placing them in spots I love around the house. Everyone has their own balance of how many family photos they prefer to display and hang within their home. For us, an old black-and-white photo of my grandma and grandpa sits on our living room table, prompting a smile and the sweet memories of walking through their front door when I was a child. Enlarged, framed family prints are on DIY ledges we made, and it fills my heart with joy to see those special moments of our family. Our apothecary cabinet holds vintage frames displaying interchangeable family photos.

We all have cozy memories with the ones we love, so why not display them? Hang collections of treasured photos on a gallery wall, rotating them by season, occasion, or simply a whim. Style in frames on bookshelves and tables. Or gather into albums and keep close by for slow walks down memory lane. No matter the season, be sure to include this coziest of details in your home.

SUMMER
NO.
42
TIP

COZY OUTDOORS

I've found that time outside refreshes and rejuvenates my soul. I benefit so much from the fresh air and vitamin D, and when I create a cozy spot outside, I am more likely to take advantage of them. If you don't currently have a cozy space outdoors, I highly recommend giving it a try and creating your very own escape from the chaos. A porch or patio retreat—even a cozy spot under the trees—can provide much-needed moments of relaxation and escape, which makes for your very own staycation.

Whether your space is a traditional patio, a backyard deck, a tiny apartment balcony, or a nearby park, it's a space to slip away to at the end of the day with your favorite drink—or to start off the morning with a cup of your favorite brew. It may take a bit of extra creativity, but regardless of the size of your space or the size of your budget, you can create your own cozy outdoor escape with these essentials:

Seating and cushions: Depending on your space and budget, this might be a single chair, a wrought-iron patio set, or an entire suite of outdoor furniture. Add outdoor pillows and cushions to ensure seating is comfortable and cozy. Consider your family's size and the activities that will happen in the space to help you choose just the right pieces.

Table: Match the size to your seating—a tiny table for a single chair or larger ones for more seating. Bring your creativity into play and think outside the box. Coat a wooden dining table with outdoor paint, or use an upturned galvanized trough for a unique coffee table. Look around. What other unique items can you repurpose for your outdoor space? A coat of paint or clear varnish will help them survive the elements. Or leave the pieces just as they are for a weathered look.

Shade: Summer's soaring temperatures beg for shady spots. Add umbrellas to provide an escape from the heat. Look for adjustable ones that tilt to follow—and block—the sun. For patios, consider installing a sun sail or pergola, or add outdoor ceiling fans to covered porches to bring cool breezes.

Lighting: Strings of sophisticated Edison-style bulbs or simple twinkle lights lend outdoor areas a cozy, welcoming glow. Place lanterns of metal or wicker on tabletops and in corners, or hang from a post or nearby tree. And don't forget to keep a few citronella candles on hand to chase away pesky bugs.

Outdoor rugs: Cover rough decks and concrete patios with outdoor rugs. They not only create gathering spots for conversation, they also are cozy and comfy for summertime's bare feet and toes. I like to treat my outdoor fabrics, including outdoor rugs, with a spray guard to protect them from the elements.

COZY COLLECTIONS

The art of collecting is something I excel at. It started as a child with a vast collection of Beanie Babies and I've since moved on to antique French jars, vintage book series, unique clocks, hand brooms, French market baskets, English advertising pots, and even SMEG appliances. There are so many more collections I have that I couldn't possibly list them all—those are just a few of my favorites. As you can tell, I love collecting.

I have a number of collections, almost one in every room. I love adding to them and displaying them. Without thoughtful placement, they can quickly take on the look of random clutter. And even though they may be similar in style and substance, collections can often look unrelated, misplaced, and undone.

You will never hear me say to get rid of collections—I could never comfortably part with my own. Rather, let's look at some ways to make those collections we all inevitably have just a bit cozier.

COZY TIPS FOR DISPLAYING COLLECTIONS

Group like things together.	
Gather them onto trays to give them a defined space.	
Display smaller items in glass jars or under glass cloche.	
Arrange them in baskets.	
Hang them on the walls in frames, shadow boxes, and shelves.	
Group items into a gallery wall with similar frames.	
Utilize mantels, tabletops, and shelves.	
Collect items within monochromatic color palettes.	
Display them within one shelving unit or bookcase.	
Build bookshelves to display collections (see page 110).	

No. 43

RECEIVED BY

THE ART OF TRELLISING

When it comes to creating a cozy, yet dynamic outdoor space, a trellis is high on my list. This time-tested, though often overlooked, garden addition has so much to offer. It's a wonderful way to incorporate an added element of design—both with its own structure and with the added texture of the leafy vines and climbing flowers it holds. This is how you get that cottage garden look we are all searching for.

A trellis provides a sturdy place for the young climbing rose and heavy-bloomed climbing hydrangea, for the scent-soaked clematis, and even for grapevines, sugar peas, tomatoes, or any garden plant that climbs as it grows. I especially love how the trellis can touch all five of the senses through scent, sight, touch, taste, and—if birds make their home in it—even sound.

So, are you sold on finding a spot to add a trellis yet? Consider placing one on the side of a shed, between two windows, up a chimney, by a greenhouse, or as the backdrop for a cozy outdoor space. If you are handy and love DIYs, you can easily craft your own to fit your specific area. But they can also be purchased, premade, from major retailers. For a more unique piece, check antique shops, greenhouses, and garden centers.

Trellises can come in all shapes, sizes, and materials—from garden-sized to container-sized. You'll find trellises in the standard wood and vinyl as well as some crafted from bamboo shoots, farm metal fencing, wire rope and wall anchors, primitive logs, and twine. The options are endless. If you're looking to add an element to transition from one space to another, or to create a divide or a living wall, give a trellis a try.

COZY COTTAGE PLANTS

The dreamiest little cottage is nestled in the hills of Ireland, tucked away on a small street, and covered in stone exterior with plant trellises and overgrown plant walls surrounding it. I'm always dreaming up ways to turn our house into that perfect cozy cottage, and I believe houseplants play a key role. Every vignette should have a little green in it, since adding greenery—whether faux or real—brings the cottage vibe inside.

Over time, my passion for all things growing and green has only increased. And bringing those touches of life into our home with plants soothes and grounds me in a way few other things do. Plants instantly add life, brightness, and a cozy feeling to any vignette or shelf. With a bit of trial and error along the way, I've found the ones that work best for me and my home. My hands-down favorite is pothos! Its ability to survive—even thrive—with minimal light and water, along with its tendency to curl and vine, makes this little beauty my all-time favorite houseplant.

While houseplants are generally low-maintenance, they do need a bit of attention now and then. I've listed some of my favorites that I've discovered in my "plant mom" journey.

EASY TO GROW			LOW-LIGHT PLANTS		
Aloe vera			Snake plant		
Kangaroo paw			Pothos		
Peperomia			ZZ plant		
Philodendrons			Succulents		
Snake plant			Dieffenbachia		
Succulents			Bird's-nest fern		
ZZ Plant			Maidenhair fern		

CHILD- AND PET-FRIENDLY PLANTS			TOPIARIES		
Bird's-nest fern			Lavender		
Zebra plant			Spanish lavender		
Money plant			Rosemary		
Peperomia			Angel vine		
Spider plants			Boxwood		
Staghorn fern			Olive		

No. 45

see more on
LizMarieBlog.com

COZY TIPS: TROUBLESHOOTING PLANT PROBLEMS

- If leaves are dropping, or turning yellow or brown, you may be over- or underwatering. For most plants, the soil should be damp to the touch. Avoid the extremes, and don't allow the soil to completely dry out or to be flooded when watering.

- If you need help checking the moisture of the soil, there are tools you can purchase and stick into the soil to test it.

- If gnats get in the soil, mix a tablespoon of dish soap in a spray bottle of water and lightly spray on leaves and soil. (Test on a small section first.) To prevent gnats, avoid puddling water in the bottom of planters.

- If plants get "leggy" or "spindly," they may be stretching for the sun. Try moving to a spot with more light.

SUMMERTIME BARBECUES
AND THE FOURTH OF JULY

Weekend barbecues are a great way to gather with friends and family for fun summer memories. For my American friends, the Fourth of July offers the perfect excuse for a big old summertime barbecue. Few things make me feel more at peace in the summer than being surrounded by family and friends, hearing the laughter and squeals of delighted children with sparklers, and smelling the smoke drifting off of Jose's grill.

And summertime barbecues are the

perfect excuse to bring your summer style to life outside. I like to bring out my vintage Americana baseball collection to create a cozy summer tablescape. Fill bowls and oversized jars with a collection of old baseballs. Tuck vintage flags into wicker demijohns, old glass milk bottles, pitchers, or even potted plants. This is a quick and easy way to transform a porch or patio into a nostalgic American gathering.

MY FOURTH OF JULY FAVORITES

Easy outdoor dishes: A cute set of melamine plates is a good outdoor option, but if your crowd is big, and you need to go with disposable, I prefer using white, heavy-duty paper plates.

Sand buckets and sparklers: You're never too old for sparklers! Little bouquets of sparklers in sand buckets are easy to pass out to guests, and the sand buckets are a safe spot to return them to.

Ice-cold drinks: Fill a vintage cooler or ice buckets with your favorite drink. Some things we keep in ours are sodas,

flavored water, seltzers, and our guests' favorite drinks!

Yard games: Who doesn't love a competitive game of cornhole or bocce ball?

On the grill: It's all about the grill; for our barbecues we love grilled tapas, kabobs, and Mexican street corn. Don't forget to mix in the fresh fruits and vegetables from your garden!

SUMMER
NO.
47
TIP

MAKE YOUR OWN
CLOTHESLINE

When I think of a farmhouse with a clothesline in the backyard, I think of the perfect mixture of form and function. If you have had linens or blankets dried by the sun, then you know the next level of cozy that brings into any space. If you already have two trees or two posts where you could hang a clothesline in your yard, then you're almost done! You'll just need a few items, such as clothesline rope and clothesline tighteners. Otherwise, visit LizMarieBlog.com and follow the plans to build your own.

Not only will a clothesline save on dryer time, but it will also add a touch of old-fashioned cozy to your laundry days. For an extra touch of freshness, plant a grouping of lilacs nearby or along the base of each clothesline.

COZY TIP: KIDS' FUN WITH CLOTHESLINES

Did you know that a clothesline is for more than just drying clothes and linens? With the drape of a sheet or two, it also makes the perfect summertime fort for little ones. Throw a blanket on the ground underneath, and it becomes a shady spot for picnics, reading, or even an afternoon nap. With mini projects being more popular and affordable, turn your picnic setting into a spontaneous movie night under the stars.

BUILT-IN SHELVES

I love every project we do, but I'm particularly happy with the finished results of this one. It looks harder than it actually is. These built-in shelves are so easy to make and are the prettiest way to store home décor. Plus, it's a great summer project so you're ready for back to school and some cozy book time indoors with the coming fall and winter.

Built-in shelves are a great use of a blank wall in your home that you don't know what to do with. I love using ours to store décor, but you could style these shelves any way you'd like. Storage can be difficult to come by in smaller homes, but with floor-to-ceiling shelves, you are utilizing the space to its fullest. It provides so much additional storage that's crucial in smaller spaces. And these built-in shelves can be added to so many different areas—the end of a hallway, an office, kids' rooms, the attic, bonus room, mudroom, bathroom, and more. If you are looking for some quick and easy built-ins that are not

only functional but can serve as a backdrop for a space, visit LizMarieBlog.com for instructions on how to do this great cozy project.

FALL

FALL

At White Cottage Farm, fall is the season for savoring and for soaking up those last bits of warmth before winter rushes in. After the heat of summer, I'm ready for refreshing walks in the brisk morning air and for cozying up to the fire on chilly evenings. It's time to layer on a comfy sweater, pull on my favorite pair of boots, and pull out that cozy hat that's been beckoning to me for weeks. I look forward to wandering through a corn maze with Jose and Cope and snapping pictures in a pumpkin patch. I anticipate the joy of teaching Cope how to pick apples from the orchard and watching as he relishes that first crisp crunch of fruit, fresh off the tree.

In our home, the line between indoors and outdoors fades even more as pumpkins, gourds, and branches of brightly colored leaves adorn shelves and tabletops and spill out onto porch steps and patios. Days are filled with collecting the last of the harvest, and evenings are spent gathering with family and friends around the fireside. It's fall—colorful, rich, savor-every-last-drop fall. And it's time to get cozy.

FALL DÉCOR

With its rich colors and abundance of textures, fall—perhaps more than any other season—calls out to me to use its natural beauty in my décor. It's those elements of the outdoors that form the foundation of my autumn decorating, along with a few cozy pillows and throws, of course. As the days grow shorter and temperatures grow milder, I wander through our home, gradually replacing summer's blooms.

As you venture forth into fall, consider incorporating some of these staples into your home décor.

Pumpkins and gourds: Pick up a few traditional pumpkins, but be sure to also toss in a few bumpy, squat, and crooked-neck gourds in all the colors and sizes.

Rich pillows and poufs: Think soft-to-the-touch velvets in fall's jewel tones, neutral knitted pillows, or rich, earth-toned faux furs. Rather than invest in new pillows each season, opt for pillow covers that are not only less expensive but also easier to store.

Warm throws: The cozier, the better. Drape them over couches, chairs, and benches. Toss one on the foot of the bed for those nights when temperatures dip a bit lower. Choose throws specific to the colors of fall or neutral tones that can be used season after season.

Wood and wicker elements: Woven baskets, wicker demijohns, and wooden bowls add a beautiful touch of texture, while also providing a place to gather all those lovely fall stems.

Bottles, jars, and crockery: Look for patinaed glass bottles and jars tinted in autumn hues. Group on tables, shelves, or in an old wooden tray—alone or intertwined with seasonal stems and pumpkins.

FALL WARDROBE STAPLES

It's time for crunching leaves on afternoon walks, laughing around the campfire, and hunting for the biggest pumpkin in the patch. In Michigan, autumn often brings dramatic changes in temperature, varying as much as forty degrees or more in the same day. So, this season calls for all the layers—snuggly, long-sleeved tees and sweatshirts, cozy sweaters and plaid shirt jackets, and, of course, boots! Here are some of my fall favorites.

Long-sleeved tees: Perfect alone or for layering, this essential piece can easily be dressed up for casual events or dressed down. I love them in basic black, gray, and white, but pops of rust, camel, and evergreen add variety to my layering.

Sweatshirts: Today's sweatshirts are endlessly stylish and cozy. They're perfect for around the house, but paired with the right jeans or leggings, they can be worn just about anywhere.

Cardigans and sweaters: Bring out all of the cozy sweaters when fall rolls around. I love neutral-colored sweaters in all different styles. Cardigans offer the perfect layering piece so you don't have to bring out your heavier jackets quite yet!

Scarves: Scarves can add warmth without bulk, making them the perfect layering pieces for fall. Choose long, drapey ones in neutral-colored knits or autumn-toned favorites.

Boots: Fall is the perfect time to pull out your favorite booties! I love a low-heel bootie, which can be worn with multiple outfits, from super-casual to dressy.

Hats: Neutral and full of style—that's what I'm looking for in a hat. Toss one on to add an instant touch of flair. Fall is the perfect season for all the hats.

Fragrance: Autumn's cozy, cooling temps have me reaching for fragrances a bit more earthy and rich, with hints of vanilla, orange blossom, and amber. My go-to is Carlen Parfums Butch Femme.

FALL STEMS

So often we think of florals as being for the spring and summer months, but I find them to be an essential part of cozy décor all year, adding life, movement, height, and texture. For fall, I like to choose from beautiful sunflowers, floaty wheatgrass stems, or one of my favorites—fall branches I've foraged from the farm. And don't forget about all the pumpkins, gourds, and even fall fruits that can bring a touch of the cozy, colorful outdoors into your home. In addition to trying out faux and fresh, fall is a great time to experiment with dried florals.

Anchor collections of gourds and pumpkins with leafy greenery, bunches of kale, or sphagnum moss, and tuck into

WHITE COTTAGE FARM

FAVORITE FALL OPTIONS

Apples		
Branches of fall leaves		
Foliage that speaks to your style and location		
Gourds		
Kale		
Leafy garlands		
Mums		
Pears		
Pumpkins		
Sunflowers		

Mix real and faux for the best look!

FAVORITE DRIED OPTIONS

Ammobium		
Cornstalks		
Eucalyptus		
Globe amaranth		
Grass varieties		
Hydrangeas		
Lavender		
Wildflowers		

No. 51   see more on
                              LizMarieBlog.com

corners, under benches, and on shelves. Mix faux fruit, preferably with stems and leafy branches still attached, for a beautiful centerpiece. Or pile collections of seasonal apples and pears into wooden bowls or creamy white crockery—this makes for a beautiful display.

And don't forget the garlands! Drape leafy, colorful garlands over mantels, weave them into your vignettes, or wrap them around wreaths for instant color and autumn cozy.

Whether I'm gathering pumpkins at a pumpkin patch on a crisp fall day or getting lost in the creativity and experience of arranging fresh, fragrant stems, I try to stop and savor the peace of these moments. Cozy is not about rushing but about living.

FALL
NO.
52
TIP

COZY APPLE BAR

Fall is the season for enjoying freshly picked apples. Whether it's for a casual gathering of family, a birthday party, or simply a fun afternoon snack, I love setting up an apple bar with all the options.

Start by slicing apples to serve in bowls or on skewers. (Toss with a little lemon juice, pineapple juice, or ginger ale to keep them from browning.) Fill additional bowls with gooey caramel, marshmallow fluff, melted milk chocolate, or white chocolate. Be sure to offer plates of toppings to dip the fruit in—sprinkles, chopped nuts, graham cracker crumbs, coconut flakes, or bits of chopped chocolate candies. Guests can then choose their base and create their own fresh, flavorful masterpiece.

DECORATIVE PLATE RACK

I love plates, dishes, and serving trays because they so perfectly exhibit beautiful form and function. Whether I'm buying new dishes or vintage antique ones, I look for pieces that can be used for food service and also serve as décor in our kitchen and dining spaces. Because when I find a new or vintage beauty, of course I'm going to want to display it!

Jose built me this beautiful plate rack, and this DIY is another completely customizable project you can adjust to fit your needs. This wall-length rack stores and displays so much for us, but if you have room even for one shelf, it can be a cute asset to your kitchen.

First determine both your wall space and the size of the dishes you want to display. This could be built as a separate piece you hang on the wall, or you can build it directly onto the wall. Here a few ways to customize your piece:

- Do you want the back to be your painted wall or a different pattern or texture, like wallpaper or bead board?

- Make sure you have a bottom lip and a plate rail half the height of your plates to keep them from falling. Note that the rails can be rustic boards, industrial metal, or fancy trim.

- If you make your bottom shelf board a bit deeper, you can add interesting hooks to hang greens, baskets, or decorative tea towels.

APPLE CIDER BAR

Perhaps it's because I always want a beverage in my hand or nearby, but I believe offering drinks to our guests is a staple of the cozy life. That's why Jose and I love creating beverage bars whenever we have family or friends over. Creating a delicious custom drink becomes an experience to share together. The drinks vary with the season, and for fall it has to be apple cider. Whether you like it hot or cold, here are my go-to recipes.

HOT APPLE CIDER BAR

This is a basic recipe to get you started, but you can mix and match and experiment to create your own favorites (see more options below). *Makes approximately 8 servings.*

Ingredients

8 cups apple cider

3 cinnamon sticks

8 whole cloves

8 allspice berries

1 orange

1 lemon

1 apple, sliced, divided

3 tablespoons brown sugar

Additional cinnamon sticks, for garnish

Instructions

1. Pour apple cider into a large saucepan.
2. Gather the cinnamon sticks, cloves, allspice, lemon and orange peels, and half of the apple slices into a square of cheesecloth and tie into a bundle.
3. Add the bundle of fruit and spices to the cider, stir in the brown sugar, then heat to a boil, and reduce heat to simmer for 5 to 10 minutes.
4. Serve warm, garnished with remaining apple slices and cinnamon sticks.

COLD APPLE CIDER BAR

Pour cold apple cider into a drink dispenser. Allow guests to fill their cups and add garnishes and fruits of their choice.

SPICE OPTIONS	FRUIT OPTIONS	GARNISH OPTIONS
Cinnamon sticks	Orange slices	Cinnamon sticks
Nutmeg	Lemon slices	Caramel
Whole cloves	Apple slices	Star anise
Allspice berries	Cranberries	Cranberries
Star anise	Pear slices	Allspice berries
Pumpkin spice	Pomegranates	Whipped cream

FALL BUCKET LIST

There's nothing like the crisp, cooling weather of fall to beckon me outdoors. It's that perfect time of year—not too hot and not too chilly—for making memories. Here are just a few of my favorite must-dos for the season. What's on your list?

WHITE COTTAGE FARM

FALL BUCKET LIST

Wander through a corn maze.	Go to a county fair.
Eat all things pumpkin.	Go foraging in a forest.
Take a hayride.	Visit a fall festival or flea market.
Decorate the porch for fall.	Make an apple cider bar.
Take in a drive-in movie or spooky movie night.	Decorate for Halloween and go trick-or-treating.
Carve pumpkins and roast pumpkin seeds.	Go apple picking and enjoy an apple fresh off the tree.
Preserve or can something from fall's harvest.	Rake up a big pile of leaves and then jump in.
Grab a favorite fall drink and spend a Saturday antiquing.	Go to a bonfire, or build one of your own and invite others to join you.
Go leaf-peeping to find all of the changing colorful fall foliage.	Try a new recipe—cozy soups and slow-cooker meals are the best.
Pick out the perfect pumpkin at a pumpkin patch.	Share memories and stories of all the things you're grateful for.

No. 55

RECEIVED BY

HAPPY HALLOWEEN

"When witches go riding, and black cats are seen, the moon laughs and whispers 'tis near Halloween."

MAKE YOUR OWN ANTIQUE ART

I love when I'm out antiquing and the perfect piece of art catches my eye. These antique pieces draw me in, and I have so many featured around our home. Each piece tells me a story, and their aged patina adds yet another layer of cozy.

While every room could benefit from such a piece of character-creating art, authentic antique art can be hard to find at affordable prices. Thankfully, there are websites where digital art files can be purchased and then printed on canvas, paper, or cardstock. Add a vintage-looking frame, and they're ready to hang. Or you could DIY your own vintage art to create the perfect piece for your cozy home.

Or for an even quicker pop of creativity, display art on your flat screen.

HOW TO MAKE YOUR OWN ANTIQUE ART

Materials:

printout of a piece of digital art
canvas, in the same size as the art
spray adhesive

paper towels
antiquing wax or stain (optional)

How to:

1. Select a piece of digital art and print it out on a piece of paper, either on your own home printer or at any print center. Thinner paper is best for this project, and standard printer paper works as well.

2. Use spray adhesive to adhere the printed piece to a canvas of the same size. Once the paper is on the canvas, gently rub out the bubbles.

3. Using a wet paper towel, rub the edges of the printed paper outward. This will wear down the edges and spread the ink to add a patina-like effect. At this point, you can choose to add more wear to the print using the wet paper towel, or simply allow it to dry.

4. Once dry, seal your art with an antiquing wax or stain. You can even sand down areas to make it look truly antique.

The Lord is my shepherd; I shall not want. He makes me to lie down in green pastures; He leads me beside the still waters; He restores my soul; He leads me in the paths of righteousness for His name's sake. Yea, though I walk through the valley of the shadow of death, I will fear no evil, for You are with me; Your rod and Your staff they comfort me. You prepare a table before me in the presence of my enemies; You anoint my head with oil; My cup runs over. Surely goodness and mercy shall follow me all the days of my life, and I will dwell in the house of the Lord forever

SEASONAL COLOR PALETTES

By keeping my walls white and my everyday foundation décor neutral and year-round cozy, changing to the palette of the season becomes easy to achieve. Seasonal décor can seem overwhelming, but we love that our neutral home offers a great starting point and base to work from.

My number one tip for keeping my seasonal décor collection in check is to choose a color palette. Personally, I love subdued earth tones—think earthy greens, subtle ambers, and muted rusts. To help determine your palette, find a fall fabric, pillow, or item that speaks to you most. Or take a walk outside to discover nature's fall palette.

Don't forget about wood tones. More than just a texture, wood also brings so much color and warmth to any room. When searching for wood pieces for our home, I tend to favor antique pine. I love the light, natural tone of the wood, and the worn texture amps up the cozy factor.

When it comes to incorporating your seasonal color palette, consider those things that aren't permanent fixtures in your home—items that can easily be switched out for the seasons. Stems and greenery, pillows, throws, tablecloths, and tea towels are great ways to bring the color palette into your home. Then think beyond that to your shelf décor, artwork, rugs, pots, and vases. There are endless ways to incorporate seasonal colors into your home. Do what's best for your cozy style.

DISPLAY YOUR OWN ART

I mentioned before how I love antique art pieces and unique art finds for our home; however, those can get a bit pricey. One way to add a really custom touch to your home is to create and display your own artwork. Find a piece that really inspires you and re-create something similar, or if you are feeling brave, dive straight into creating a truly unique piece. There are so many different mediums to use depending on your personal style: watercolors, charcoal, acrylic paint, graphite, pastels, photography, and more. To blend these custom art pieces into your décor, frame them, incorporate them into vignettes, and display them proudly. To keep things fresh, I switch out my artwork with the seasons and with new creations. Look for unique antique frames in all shapes and sizes to display art creations.

Not only can you display your own art this way, but it is also a great way to display your children's art. Our son's imagination and creations are part of the story of our home. I feel it's important to honor and encourage our children's creative wanderings. One way to do that is to invite your children to be a part of your decorating efforts. Simply give them a canvas and some paints that match your color scheme and see what wonderfulness they create. Demonstrating to our children that their imagination and efforts matter to us does more to create a cozy home than any pillow or throw ever could.

COZY TIP

Feeling overwhelmed with your child's artwork and school papers? One of my tips is to save all of their artwork throughout the year in a box or basket, then go through the art together at the end of the year to decide what to keep.

FALL
NO.
59
TIP

FALL PORCH AND STEPS

I go all out when it comes to our fall porch and try color combinations that fully represent the season. For me, this is the area to experiment with nature and let that influence the end result.

The colors of fall make this so easy to do. My go-to secret is to fill this space with pumpkins and gourds. Pile and stack them, as if they're spilling down the steps and overflowing from the garden. Add in a few knobby and multicolored gourds, dried cornstalks, and mounds of mums, and you're well on your way to an epic fall scene. Pots of colorful cabbages add even more color and texture.

To make supplies more affordable, we grow our own pumpkins and go to local farmers for our fall porch décor. If you don't want to grow your own, I highly recommend shopping local to get the best deals. Over the years, we've developed great relationships with local farms, and oftentimes they will offer deals when buying a larger quantity of pumpkins and gourds. Prices vary based on location and the availability of pumpkins in your area.

I also love incorporating rustic metals with galvanized buckets, watering cans, and vintage metal planters. Pack them with mums or gourds—or both. Choose items that inspire you, and add them to your porch. This is the perfect spot to experiment and try something out of the box with your décor.

COZY TIPS TO KEEP PUMPKINS FROM ROTTING

- Give them a good scrub with dish soap or bleach, as rot and moldy patches usually get their start under the bits of dirt and debris.

- Spray a clear coat of polyurethane to make them last all season long. (The polyurethane also helps to deter creatures from eating your pumpkins.)

CHARMING PEGS AND HOOKS

I love the simplicity and usefulness of a basic peg rail, one with shelves, or even wall hooks. If you've followed me for any length of time, you've probably seen them in my kitchen, entry, and mudroom. This is a relatively easy DIY if you love a good project (search "peg rail" on LizMarieBlog. com), or they can be found online through a variety of retailers.

Peg rails and hooks are décor staples that add both form and function to your home and come in enough varieties that they can offer a timeless, vintage vibe or fit in a space with modern simplicity. Some of the best places to hang them are in the kitchen, bathroom, mudroom, entryway, or closet.

I would describe my peg rail and hook décor as a beautiful paradox. Traditionally utilitarian items would not be proudly displayed as décor. However, if the practical items you own are pretty to look at and match your personal style, they can serve as décor as well. By styling these items, they become readily available and help to prevent you from overbuying items that serve only one purpose. We often spend money on both useful and beautiful items, but what if you could buy one item that is useful and beautiful? I found that peg rails are the perfect way to do this and have styled them in our home.

THE HISTORY OF PEG RAILS

Peg rails are used in a lot of historic homes. I fell in love with the look of them and knew I wanted them in our home. The peg originated with the Shakers as a simple but ingenious way to keep houses organized. It allows you to keep items off the floors and instead hung on the walls. Simply tidy up your home by corralling all items into one spot.

WHITE COTTAGE FARM

Here are some of my favorite things to hang on pegs and hooks, and shelves if they have them.

Robes	Coats	Blankets
Bath towels	Hats	Baskets
Hand towels	Scarves	Tea towels
Loofah scrubber	Seasonal gear	Measuring cups
Bag hamper	Purses or totes	Pretty mugs
Necklaces	Bags	Cutting boards
Crocks of wooden spoons	My favorite pair of scissors	White enamel colanders

No. 60

see more on
LizMarieBlog.com

ADDING TEXTURE TO WALLS

When I think of decorating a room or a space, the walls receive a large part of my attention. Not just the color, but the texture as well. Texture is a key way to instantly bring a historic look into your home, and my goal with our house has been to restore it to its original character. For me, the more texture, the better.

Yet the walls of so many of our homes are lacking in texture. Most are simple drywall, perhaps with a bit of crown molding or a chair rail. So what do you do when your walls are smooth but you long for cozy texture? Create your own. And these days, there are more options than ever before. Many are affordable and offer relatively easy installation. To determine which texture is right for you and your space, start with this simple exercise.

Imagine you are in a room with an exposed brick wall. Perhaps it stands alone or surrounds a fireplace. How do you feel in that room? Now imagine a wall of shiplap.

Its clean lines flow from one side of the room to the other. How cozy does that room feel?

Curious about other options? Imagine painting that brick white—either solid or leaving some of the original color peeking through. Or instead of cleanly hung shiplap, imagine mixed and matched boards of varying lengths, tongue and groove, or beadboard.

There is no right or wrong answer when it comes to texture. Go for what appeals to you and makes you feel cozy. That's the texture you should explore for your space. Before you get started, let's take a closer look at the options for adding texture.

Shiplap: This product has been so popular in recent years. Shiplap comes in a number of different wall coverings in a wide variety of shapes, sizes, colors, and materials. Nickel slot (or nickel gap) tongue and groove features boards that, when nested together, leave a nickel-edge-wide gap between each board. All edges are squared. There is also V-groove tongue and groove. When nested together, these boards create a V line that emphasizes where the boards meet. Of course, you could always cut your own wood or plywood planks and stack them up the wall, allowing them to touch or leaving space in between.

Beadboard or vertical shiplap: Beadboard can come in sheets or panels, but we prefer to install our beadboard with tongue-and-groove planks, similar to shiplap. In our experience it is much easier to work with these pieces on a smaller scale for large rooms and for cutting around objects like outlets and switches.

The most important thing when hanging wall covering vertically rather than horizontally—as you would see with traditional shiplap—is to ensure you are nailing each plank to a surface that will

hold the vertical plank. The advantage of hanging shiplap horizontally is that it runs perpendicular to the wall studs, allowing you to nail along the shiplap plank where it crosses a stud. When hanging the shiplap or beadboard vertically, you are running with the studs, or in parallel, so there are areas where there is structurally nothing to attach the plank to the wall.

If you have drywall already installed with a traditionally framed wall, meaning that studs are vertically installed roughly sixteen inches on center (give or take based on location and age of home), you will need to create a backer board of some sort to run horizontally for the beadboard to be attached to. Here are three different ways to attach beadboard or vertical ship-lap to the wall. As always when installing any wall treatment that requires nailing, properly identify any electrical, HVAC, and plumbing before cutting and nailing. You can do this with a stud finder that has features to identify studs and other items. Also, visually check if there are registers and vents along the path.

1. Horizontally remove sections of drywall in "strips" roughly 4 feet apart. This will expose the face of the studs and openings between each stud. You can place backers between them horizontally so you can attach the vertical planks.

2. Completely remove the drywall in the sections where you are installing the vertical planks, and install the horizontal 2x4s (backers) 4 feet apart in each of the openings between the studs.

3. If you are like us and already have horizontal shiplap installed on the front of studs, they will hold any vertical shiplap or beadboard in place, being a perfect backer board.

Brick veneer: This popular method of adding texture uses thinly cut pieces of brick. They can be made from real bricks or manufactured materials. Veneers are installed using mastic to adhere the brick to the wall and mortar to fill in the gaps. Once installed, the veneer will look like an actual brick wall.

Wallpaper: The best update to wallpaper was making it easily removable. Oftentimes we consider wallpaper to be a long-term wall texture, but with the ease of removable wallpaper, you can add this to any space to create instant cozy texture in a room. This is a great option for anyone who is renting a home or apartment—you can add this custom touch but easily remove it when or if you have to move.

Wall texture is the base of a room; it's the foundation of styling your space and is as important as the furniture you put into a room. Whether you decide to add beadboard or wallpaper, this sets the tone for the style. A change like this can completely transform the way your space looks and feels and can be achieved at all different budgets depending on how much work you want to do yourself.

FORAGING FOR FALL FINDS

So often when we think of décor, we think of what we should buy and where we should shop. But over the years, I've learned to turn my thoughts first to what I can collect from the farm and forest around me. There I find so many of the lovely natural elements that create a cozy addition to vignettes, shelves, vases, baskets, and mantels. They add color and life and texture, perfectly reflecting whatever season we're in, but especially autumn, with its dried grasses, falling leaves, and piles of pinecones.

As the days turn chilly and leaves begin to transform, I grab a basket and my favorite cutting shears, and Cope and I go exploring. Seeing nature through his eyes calls to mind so many possibilities—treasures I might have otherwise overlooked. His little fingers find pinecones and acorns, interesting bits of bark and moss, and curiously shaped stones. Into the basket they all go.

As we walk, I search for slim branches of interesting shapes, perhaps with leaves still attached. I might find a few late-blooming flowers to fill a vase or two. I'll even collect some mushrooms and lichen to dry and tuck into vignettes. (A quick online search will help you choose which ones to collect and which can be poisonous. Always keep them away from little ones.) Once our treasures are found, we head home to display them. Cope gets his own special place to arrange his finds, somewhere he can see them and know that his choices matter to me.

Nature is a huge inspiration for me when I'm styling our home. Through foraging I find so many incredible items that help me bring the outdoors in. As you decorate, think of ways to bring these foraged items in—you'd be surprised at what goodies you can find in your own backyard. Or visit a local or state park. Be sure to check their guidelines first, but many will allow you to forage to your heart's content when it's simply for your own use. My best advice when foraging—whatever the season—is to relax, to wander, and to let the possibilities unfold before you.

WHITE COTTAGE FARM

HERE ARE SEVERAL WAYS I DISPLAY OUR DISCOVERIES

- Fill jars on shelves
- Gather items in vintage stoneware
- Arrange branches into vases
- Press leaves for frames
- Create centerpieces for the table or kitchen island
- Hang wildflower bundles from peg rails

No. 62

see more on
LizMarieBlog.com

BEING PRESENT IN ALL SEASONS

The greatest secret to living the cozy life has nothing to do with picking paint colors, layering the bed just so, or creating the perfect seasonal vignette. It doesn't require color-coordinating, rearranging, tweaking, or fluffing. So what is this secret to living the cozy life? It's simply this: be present.

One of the greatest pieces of advice I've ever been given came from a mentor when I asked this question: How do you keep balance in your life? The answer was this: In whatever you are doing, be all there. In other words, don't let your body be in one place, while your thoughts are somewhere entirely different. When you are at work, be fully at work in your mind and actions. When you are at home eating dinner with your loved ones, be all there. When you are at your child's soccer game, be there. And when you are allowing yourself a break from all the demands of life, be there also. The other things can usually wait until later.

Our coziest moments are the ones where we are most fully present.

WOODEN STEP STOOL

All projects and DIYs seem to leave behind scrap pieces of wood, which are simply too valuable to throw away. So, like most people, we save and store those pieces to use for future projects.

One of my favorites is this step stool built completely from leftover wood. Whether you use scraps or wood cut specifically for this project, this lovely little stool will make a cozy—and useful—addition to your home. Visit LizMarieBlog.com for the full set of instructions to make this particular stool.

Or make a super-simple partial DIY stool with that same leftover scrap wood by cutting the board to size and adding screw-in legs of your choice.

Either way, stools are not only practical for reaching greater heights or for an added seat, but they also serve as great plant stands to add height and dimension.

FALL
NO.
65
TIP

CLEANING ANTIQUES

I love using antiques at home, but they don't always arrive in the greatest condition. Here are my best tips and tricks for cleaning your new-to-you treasures.

Before you buy: Open drawers and doors to look for signs of animal nests or holes from bugs. Do a smell test to check for any odd odors. Look at the back and underneath for damage or other warning signs, like mold and mildew.

Wood furniture: Wipe with a dry cloth to remove dust and grime, then wipe with a wet cloth and mild cleaner. For stuck-on grime, steel wool or a bristle brush work well. Once the dirt and grime have been removed, dry with a clean rag. Spray with furniture polish, if you like. If it's super dirty, don't be afraid to pressure wash it.

Chippy Paint: Use a blow dryer or leaf blower to remove dust. Then, use a damp cloth to remove any remaining dust. To prevent pieces of paint from continuing to fall off, use a sealer, such as polyurethane matte topcoat.

Rugs: Double vacuum to remove dirt and debris: thoroughly vacuum one side of the rug, flip it over, and then vacuum the other side. Use rug and upholstery cleaners to remove spots and stains. Wool rugs should be professionally cleaned.

Pressure washing and outdoor washing work well but are more invasive, so use this method at your own discretion and risk. Lay the rug out on a hard, flat surface. Dip a broom in hot, soapy water (I use dish soap), and scrub the soap into the rug. Use a hose or pressure washer to rinse the rug. After rinsing off the broom, use it to push the excess water out of the rug. Hang the rug to dry in the sun.

Upholstery: Use an upholstery vacuum to remove surface debris. Fabric deodorizers can often eliminate any pet smells or lingering mustiness. Upholstery cleaners are great for removing spots. Always test on a small, inconspicuous spot first.

DIY RUG AND UPHOLSTERY CLEANERS

Natural cleaners often work well. These are some of my go-to favorites. Research their use on your particular fabric, and always test on a small, inconspicuous spot. Clean to the extent your piece requires, and remember to rinse after use.

- 1/2 cup rubbing alcohol + 1/2 cup distilled white vinegar
- 1/2 cup club soda or carbonated water + 1/4 cup vinegar + 2 tablespoons dish detergent
- 1/2 cup water + 2 1/2 tablespoons vinegar

No. 65

see more on
LizMarieBlog.com

CLEANING VINTAGE METALS

Vintage metals are always unique finds when thrifting—sometimes they have the perfect amount of tarnish and wear, but other times they need cleaning to restore their look. If you choose to restore them, here are my tips for polishing them up.

Silver: To clean away tarnish, use a mild soap and warm water, then dry with a lint-free rag. If some tarnish remains, try lemon juice or olive oil.

Brass: Always wash brass pieces before polishing, in warm, soapy water, or using a soft, damp cloth. If your piece is brass-plated, you are done. (If a magnet sticks to your piece, it's brass-plated.) If the piece is brass, it will need to be polished using a polish designed specifically for brass, applied according to the instructions.

Metal: Antique metals will almost always have some kind of rust. Depending on where I want to use a piece, I might leave the rust. For severely rusted pieces, first scrub with a wire brush to remove the worst of it, followed by steel wool, and then apply mineral oil to scrub off the remaining rust. Then buff with an old rag.

WHITE COTTAGE FARM

HOMEMADE POLISH

For a homemade brass polish, mix the juice of half a lemon with a teaspoon of baking soda until it forms a paste. Apply the paste with a soft cloth. If the tarnish is heavy, let it sit for thirty minutes. Rinse with warm water and dry. Repeat, if necessary.

No. 66

see more on
LizMarieBlog.com

COZY MEASUREMENTS GUIDE

When it comes to cozy décor, there are no hard-and-fast rules. There are, however, some guidelines that I find useful. And if you need to bend—or even break—them to achieve the cozy look and feel you like, then do it. Homes should be a reflection of who we are and what we value, so don't be afraid to step outside the box and make your home truly yours in every way.

If you're trying to cozy up your space but aren't sure where to start, here are some basic measurements to help lay out your design.

Rug size for living room: Option 1: measure the size with all the legs of furniture fitting on the rug. Option 2: measure the size with all front legs of furniture fitting on the rug.

Coffee table distance from sofa and/or chairs: Place 14 to 18 inches away from each other.

Furniture distance from fireplace: At least 3 feet.

Number of pillows for sofa: For a two-seater, three to four pillows; for a three-seater, four to five pillows; and for a sectional, six to eight pillows.

Art and picture hanging height: Hang so midpoint is between 57 and 60 inches from the floor.

Chandelier and lighting heights: Hang 7 feet above ground with 8-foot-high ceilings; 8 feet above ground with higher ceilings. If hanging from a two-story ceiling, don't let it hang lower than the height of the first floor.

Curtain hanging placement: Hang 4 to 6 inches above window frame and half an inch above the ground.

TV placement: A 42-inch television should be mounted about 56 inches from floor to TV center; a 55-inch TV should be around 61 inches; a 65-inch TV should be around 65 inches; and a 70-inch television should be mounted about 67 inches to the center of the screen.

Rug size for bedroom: Option 1: measure with the entire bed frame sitting on the area rug. Option 2: Measure with entire bed frame and furniture on the area rug. Option 3: Measure with the lower two-thirds of your bed plus bench at the end of the bed on rug, but with nightstands off the rug.

Number of bed pillows: For a full-size bed, one to two for sleeping, three to five decorative. For a queen-size, two for sleeping, five to eight decorative. For a king-size and California king, two for sleeping, seven to nine decorative.

Handles on drawers: Pulls should be placed horizontally on drawers. For small drawers (less than 24 inches wide), center the knobs or pulls in both directions. On larger drawers pulls should be placed horizontally, centered at the very top of the drawer panel, where the drawer rail begins.

Handles on cabinets: On wall-mounted cabinets, knobs are usually placed 2½ to 3 inches from the bottom corner of the door. On base cabinets, they are placed 2 ½ to 3 inches from the upper corner of the door.

FALL
NO.
68
TIP

HISTORICALLY ACCURATE ELEMENTS

I love older homes and the stories they tell. We've found old bottles in the fields, tin photos and the old siding to our home in the walls, and in our laundry room we found the home's original ceiling and floors. These echoes of the past speak to my heart and make me feel rooted in this place and time.

So while I love the modern comforts, especially in the kitchen and baths, I also treasure the historical elements that truly give our century-old house its charm. Unfortunately, the remodeling efforts of previous owners mean that some of the original historical details of our home have been lost. But Jose and I are gradually restoring, re-creating, and, at times, reinventing those details.

If you're seeking to restore, re-create, or perhaps create historically accurate details in your home, begin by researching when your home was built and the styles of that time—or the styles of the time you want to re-create. Consider wall treatments, color palettes, and lighting trends. Look for the elements that most speak to your heart and go from there. Here are some of the things I consider when looking to add historically accurate details.

Paint: Use a matte finish in shades of white to be more historically accurate.

Wall treatments: Add texture with beadboard, shiplap, wallpaper, and brick.

Lighting: Look for rewired vintage lamps and chandeliers or lighting inspired by historic homes.

Corbels and other architectural salvage pieces: Paint and distress new ones, or pick up aged and chippy ones from an architectural salvage store. Use as shelf brackets, bookends, or stand-alone décor.

Stoneware: Timeless and classic, stoneware vessels are wonderful for grouping items together in a display, holding stems and blooms, or adding to vignettes.

Vintage and antique finds: Use them as their original design intended or repurpose them for something altogether different.

Vintage-inspired faucets and hardware: Use these to achieve that historically accurate look while still embracing the comforts and practicality of the modern.

Antique signs and art: Give a nod to the past by using antique signs as art for walls, mantels, and shelves.

Textiles: Antique fabric can be used for many different purposes, from curtains to tea towels to pillow covers.

Vintage furniture: Adding antique or vintage furniture pieces gives a historic touch to any room with a timeless craftsmanship that modern-day furniture can't offer.

When I can't find antique pieces for specific things in our home, I try to find something new that looks antique-inspired. All of my appliances are new and safe to use but have a vintage appearance. Any additional architectural details to your home often need to be new, but it's still possible to find ways to design them to look historic and timeless.

EASY COZY CABINET

I don't know about you, but I love a great DIY. And I love it more if it's also a creative storage solution. On more than one occasion, Jose and I have created various-sized cabinets, both mounted and freestanding, that we've used throughout our homes.

Here are two things to think about as you begin this project: Where in your home do you need pretty storage? This project is perfect for bathroom cabinets, vintage-looking kitchen pie safes, office or schoolroom bookshelves—you name it.

The second thing to think about is what kind of door you want on the cabinet. For this particular project, you'll want to identify this first. Do you have a wood-framed mirror or window? A unique vintage door? A leaded-glass beauty?

Once you've selected the cabinet door of your choice, you'll want

to carefully take measurements to figure out the height, width, and depth of the box to frame out for it. Depending on your level of skill, you may choose to add moldings, trim, or legs, so be careful to factor all of those things into your measurements.

One of my favorite things about this project is that it can be completely customized to fit your space and your style.

COZY CABINET TIPS

- Want a splash of color? Wallpaper the back wall before you put the pieces together to create an interesting statement piece.
- Paint or stain your shelves and interior walls before you put them together to make touch-up faster for hard-to-reach corners.
- If you've created a tall, free-standing cabinet, mount it to the wall for safety.
- Keep your eye out for interesting stained or leaded glass windows when you're out antiquing.
- Don't forget the hardware! Interesting knobs, pulls, and latches can be the perfect finishing touch.

No. 69

see more on
LizMarieBlog.com

HARVEST PARTY

FALL
NO.
70
TIP

Whenever possible, we move our parties outside. A cozy gathering on the patio—but still conveniently near the kitchen—is perfect for an evening grilling out with friends. Comfy chairs or simple hay bales circled around a firepit or bonfire make for wonderful conversation.

But perhaps my favorite form of outdoor entertaining is an outdoor dinner party. Just moving a table and chairs to somewhere other than the dining room instantly creates a party atmosphere and offers so many conversation starters. Sometimes we'll set up in the apple orchards, near the barn, in the open field, or just in the backyard. We might use our actual kitchen table, a table found on one of my antiquing excursions, or planks spread across wooden sawhorses. Depending on my mood, I'll leave the table bare, drape it with a patterned tablecloth, or cover it with white linen. For décor, I put my foraging skills to work, gathering leaves, branches, pumpkins, and cornstalks—whatever my surroundings have to offer.

Weave them together down the length of the table to create a casually elegant tablescape that melds perfectly with the outdoors. Keep it cozy for guests with pillows, blankets, and perhaps a fire nearby.

For food, I prefer to keep it simple with picnic-style fare and charcuterie boards laden with breads, cheese, crackers, fruits, slices of meat, and other finger foods. A cooler filled with drinks helps guests feel welcome and cared for. Look for a vintage or vintage-inspired container that brings its own touch of character to the party.

If weather or space keeps the event indoors, I've learned to change things up by simply moving our table to another room. Or I might toss a few oversized pillows on the living room floor and spread out the food on low tables. The outdoors is brought inside with those foraged finds of pinecones, leaves, and pumpkins. You'll be amazed by how a simple change of location can create a cozy atmosphere for entertaining.

WHITE COTTAGE FARM

BRING THE INDOORS OUT AND MAKE IT
AN EXTENSION OF YOUR HOME

- Throwbeds and poufs are great for seating on the ground.
- Favorite décor pieces can come outside to set the table.
- The addition of lighting to your outdoor space will allow the party to continue past dark.
- Outdoor heaters or firepits keep everyone warm on chilly days.

No. 70

see more on
LizMarieBlog.com

FALL
NO.
71
TIP

GATHERING IN GRATITUDE
AT THANKSGIVING

Thanksgiving doesn't look the same for us every single year, but over the years I've learned a few things from hosting and visiting that help the day go a little more smoothly.

If you're hosting, don't be afraid to ask for help. When everyone contributes, not only does it take the burden off of one person, but it allows everyone to share and enjoy their gifts. If you are visiting, don't be afraid to offer to help. Bring a dessert or side dish, come early to decorate, or stay later and help with the cleanup.

The coziest part of Thanksgiving is allowing ourselves and our loves to be present and taking the time to count our blessings.

FALL TABLESCAPE

I love creating cozy, seasonal tablescapes. Regardless of how simple or fancy the meal itself may be, a thoughtfully arranged tablescape is an easy way to bring the seasons into your dining room. It doesn't have to be formal, expensive, or over-the-top. Mine are often rather casual and free-flowing, featuring pieces from my many collections interspersed with the elements of nature.

Begin with a base. For fall, I prefer to use earth tones. It might be a traditional table runner, a scrunched-up tablecloth, an artfully arranged strip of vintage fabric, or even a curtain draped dramatically and asymmetrically across the table. Or I might create a base using layers of stems or greenery. Sometimes I skip this step entirely, allowing the beautiful wood of the table to be my foundation for decorating.

Next, I add height with oversized candles, slender tapers in candleholders, or vases filled with slim branches. Use bottles—clear or colorful—as inexpensive holders for candles and stems.

Finish by creating interest and adding volume by layering on gourds, pears, apples, leaves, or other foraged, natural elements. Layer, experiment, add to, and take away—this doesn't have to be a "get it right the first time" experience. Mixing and matching pieces, creating a gathering of your favorite things, as well as combining formal and natural, will give your table a timelessly cozy look.

BRING FALL TO YOUR TABLE WITH . . .

- colorful tapered candles.
- a plaid scarf or vintage plaid throw.
- real, faux, or homemade leaves out of construction paper.
- textures like jute, glass with patina, or wooden accents.
- autumn tea towels for napkins, amber bottles for candle holders, or even a scarf from your closet as a table runner.

COZY TABLESCAPE TIPS

One of my favorite Thanksgiving traditions is to create a pretty tablescape to enjoy while we're preparing the meal and gathering around the table.

- If you don't need your dining table for prep space or other meals, decorate it the day before so you don't feel rushed on Thanksgiving Day. Turn on some music and enjoy the moment.
- While you are gathering and setting up your décor and place cards, think about each person who will be joining and why you are grateful for them.
- Consider filling tiny mason jars with candy or other treats and wrapping the lids with twine and a tag as a giftable place card.
- Layer your table with things you love and that are fitting for your current season. If you have a lot of kids at the table, consider faux candles instead of real ones.
- Keep the overall height of centerpieces low so everyone can make eye contact across the table. When you gather for the meal, take turns going around the table and sharing what you are thankful for.

No. 72

see more on
LizMarieBlog.com

WINTER

WINTER

Winter is the ultimate season for all things cozy. At White Cottage Farm, it brings the quiet hush of falling snow, the scent of evergreens, and holiday gatherings with family and friends. It's the time for slowing down, bundling up, and snuggling in.

As winter blows through, we bundle with heavy layers and cozy coats. It's the farm life for us, so we're still venturing out to tend to animals and chores. In Michigan, there's lots of snow, so that means snowmen, snow angels, and snowball fights. And I am loving every moment of seeing and experiencing it all afresh through Cope's eyes.

Winter is also the season of giving, so we open our hearts and our home, and we gather—with each other, with family, with friends. Trees and greenery are wrapped with twinkling lights that blink out the message of the season. Mugs of steaming hot cocoa along with conversation and laughter chase away the chill in the air. Welcome, winter!

WINTER BUCKET LIST

Winters here at the farm can be icy cold with snow for days. But even if winters where you live are simply a milder version of summer, there are some things that just beg to be done this time of year. Here are a few of my favorite winter activities.

WHITE COTTAGE FARM

WINTER BUCKET LIST

Bake your favorite cookies.

Sip a cup of hot cocoa with all the extras.

Curl up with a cozy throw and read the day away.

Take an evening walk and search for the North Star.

Visit a Christmas tree lot to find the perfect tree.

Hang stockings by the fire.

Sing carols.

Buy new pajamas for the whole family.

Give ice skating a try.

Host a party for New Year's Eve.

Have a board game night.

Volunteer at a homeless shelter or kitchen.

Give anonymously to someone who cannot give back.

Have a cozy planning day to dream and set goals for the New Year.

No. 73

RECEIVED BY

WINTER DÉCOR STAPLES

As temperatures drop and the holiday season nears, the fresh greens and cozy whites of winter begin to replace the russets, yellows, and plums of fall. And of course, winter calls for all the cozy layers. Whether it's the main bedroom, kids' rooms, guest room, or even the couch, pile on the plush pillows and warm blankets to create the perfect spot for those essential cozy naps this time of year.

When planning winter décor, the holidays often claim the spotlight. But this coldest of seasons offers so many additional opportunities for making our homes cozy with warmth. Here are some of my must-have pieces for cozy winter decorating:

Greenery: Choose from wreaths, boughs, sprigs, garlands, and swags of pine, cedar, spruce, eucalyptus, or magnolia. Faux greenery makes decorating effortless, but consider using fresh as well—the scent is worth it.

Pinecones: Arrange them in baskets and bowls, paint them white, or simply tuck them in among the evergreens.

Layers of linens: For the coziest blankets, throws, and pillows, choose richly textured knits and soft fabrics in flannel, fleece, and faux fur. For a coordinated look, keep colors neutral with hints of bright red, cozy brown, or warm gold.

Miniature evergreens: Real or faux, these guys are a staple for winter decorating. Use them as accents in your holiday décor. But after Christmas, these little gems can handle center stage all on their own.

Containers: Moody, antique dark metal urns and vases, pots and pails create a timeless winter look, especially when mixed with fresh (or faux) evergreens. Pieces of gold and glass add a touch of sparkle to the fresh whites and greens of the season. And, of course, chippy white is always a cozy classic.

Twinkle lights: They're not just for trees, and they're not just for Christmas. Weave into garlands, wrap around trees, string along banisters and railings—inside, outside, or anywhere you want—to add a warm and welcoming glow.

WINTER STEMS

Winter decorating means greenery—and lots of it! The more and the fresher, the better. Yes, freshly cut boughs, wreaths, and branches can be a bit messy, but nothing compares to the sight and scents of fresh pine, eucalyptus, and cedar to make a winter home seem cozy. And if you happen to live a bit farther south, magnolia boughs and leaves are a perfect way to bring the outside in.

Gather greenery from your own backyard or reach out to family and friends to see if they wouldn't mind sharing a branch or two. If that's not an option, check local greenhouses, garden centers, Christmas tree lots, or big-box stores. To keep greenery fresh, place the ends in a vase of water and hide it in your decorative container. With garlands, I soak them in water before I hang them up—this helps make them last just a bit longer. Tuck bits of live greenery into your faux garlands and stems to give them an added hint of freshness. Drape over mantels and shelves, wrap around railings, tuck into corners, and arrange in vases, jars, and buckets—anywhere that needs a touch of cozy green.

WHITE COTTAGE FARM

FAVORITE FRESH OPTIONS	FAVORITE FAUX OPTIONS
Baby's breath	Christmas trees
Cedar	Eucalyptus
Eucalyptus (fresh and dried)	Pine
Magnolia	Pinecones
Pine	Poinsettia
Pinecones	Winter berry stems

No. 75

WINTER WARDROBE STAPLES

Winter temperatures in Michigan can dip into the teens and stay there for days, so I'm pulling out all the cozy things—from sweaters and jackets to scarves and heavy, warm-your-toes socks. Snow and ice call for clothes that can stand up to the cold, while glowing fireplaces beg for layers of softness. Here are some of my winter favorites:

Sweaters: I love neutral colors and classic styles, a bit oversized and perfect for staying cozy. Try to invest in well-made pieces that will last for seasons to come.

Jackets and coats: Plaid, bouclés, and heavy, cabled knits—I have an obsession with jackets and coats. Winter offers the perfect excuse for collecting these beauties. Look for both style and warmth, and choose pieces that will go with a variety of outfits in your wardrobe.

Leggings: Perfect on their own or worn under skirts and dresses for a bit of extra warmth, leggings are a versatile and essential piece of my winter wardrobe. Black leggings pair well with sweaters, jackets, and cardigans. You can even find them fleece-lined for that extra cozy touch.

Loungewear: Winter's blustery winds keep us spending more time indoors. I love curling up by a fire with a soft throw and my coziest loungewear. Choose move-with-you tops and bottoms in soft-to-the-touch fabrics to stay comfy and warm.

Waterproof boots and shoes: Whether you're traipsing around a farm or just headed to the car, choose boots or shoes that will keep your feet warm and dry.

Scarves, hats, and mittens: A quick walk around the farm, and you'll quickly realize these accessories are essential. I love hand-knitted pieces in chunky yarns. Gloves are great for driving and working outside, but mittens keep fingers toasty warm!

Fragrance: For winter, I like Glossier You eau de parfum. Although it can be worn any time of year, it's the perfect scent for this season, with its woodsy, slightly sweet scent that comes from ambrette seeds and warm, ambery ambrox.

A COZY LAYERED BED

Nothing says cozy quite like the look and feel of a layered bed, and there are a few simple things I've learned that can help anyone achieve that designer look.

Overstuff: For your duvet cover and your pillow covers, overstuff them both! For the duvet you want to size up on your inserts if you can, and sometimes, I even like to use two inserts to overstuff the duvet. For the pillow covers you want to do the same. Use an insert one size larger than the pillow cover, or just go ahead and stuff two in there.

Choose down: When selecting inserts, choose down feather or down alternative when you can. Down feather is usually fluffier and keeps its shape and fullness longer. It even has hypoallergenic options, but if that's a concern, there are a lot of down alternatives with plenty of fluff.

Stick with Euro: One of my favorite bed-making secrets is to use Euro pillow covers. They are larger than most accent pillows, which makes the bed look fuller but less crowded. Imagine the difference between a bed with three large Euro pillows compared to one with several smaller 20 x 20 or 18 x 18 pillows. Euro pillows make the bed look cozy because they are large statement pieces—perfect for leaning against with your favorite book.

Layer the bedding: The final key to that designer bed is to layer your bedding. I typically layer with a mattress topper, fitted sheet, top sheet, woven blanket, fleece blanket, and duvet or comforter, and then top it off with a throw or quilt. I expose all the layers, with the final one being the duvet folded toward the bottom of the bed. I love a slightly undone, cozy look to the bed so it's ready to hop in at the end of the day.

As with everything cozy, it's important to make this work for you. Choose layers you love that help you sleep well. Layer them and fold them back so you can effortlessly climb into bed at night.

WINTER NO. 78 TIP

CHRISTMAS COOKIE DECORATING TRADITION

Is it just me, or do cookies seem even better in the winter and holiday season? Especially when they're fresh out of the oven and paired with a cup of steaming hot cocoa.

Baking cookies is something I remember doing at Christmas baking parties throughout my childhood with our family. And now it's a tradition I want to share with Cope. Yes, baking with a toddler is a little messy, but that smile is even yummier than the cookies and well worth any mess. Whether it's for your own family, extended family and friends, or even simply for yourself, host a cookie baking party.

Decide on your guests. Then choose your favorite recipe, or two, or three. (Or buy slice-and-bake! Whatever works for you.) When it comes to cookies, the more the merrier, right? Gather all the tools and ingredients, and let the baking begin. Invite guests to join you for the baking process, or prebake cookies and let guests join you in the decorating.

Now, it's probably no surprise that one of my favorite parts of baking cookies is the decorating. And it's also probably no surprise that I like to have lots of options. Fill bowls with goodies for guests to choose from.

SOME OF MY FAVORITES ARE:

- crushed candy canes
- sprinkles
- piping bags filled with icing
- small, colorful candies for eyes, noses, and buttons
- melted almond bark and chocolate for dipping

Decorating cookies can be a sticky business, so consider providing aprons for your guests. Then send them home with their creations tucked into cellophane cookie bags topped with a copy of the recipe and a bright-red bow.

ORGANIZING THE LAUNDRY ROOM

I like to tackle my major organizing during different seasons so I'm not trying to do everything all at once. Winter is great for taking on smaller areas, like the laundry room. Since laundry is necessary, I say we should make it as cozy and as beautiful as possible. That's my philosophy about most things in life. We generally spend a lot of time in our laundry rooms, so here are some ideas to keep them functional and enjoyable.

Start by taking stock of your space and assessing how it's working for you:

- Are detergents and other supplies easy to reach?
- Is there room for laundry baskets, hangers, and hampers?
- What do you need to change to make the space really work for you?

Some things are, of course, dictated by the available space. Consider how you might work in one or more of these additions to make your space truly functional:

- A shelf or cabinets over the washer and dryer for storage.
- A drying rack for delicates and handwash items. If space is tight, try a fold-down rack that mounts on the wall, or use a cute laundry ladder.
- A table or counter for folding clothes.
- A rod for extra hangers and a place to let clothes hang dry.

Once you've addressed the way the space works for you, have some fun with how it looks. Approach this space just as you would any other room in your home to make it both useful and beautiful.

- Switch out clunky, commercial packaging in favor of pretty but useful containers. Powdered detergents store prettily in wide-mouthed, clear glass jars. Drop in a shiny silver scoop for measuring.

🜋 A galvanized or enamel bin will store dryer sheets or dryer balls and is easy to dust and keep clean.

🜋 Pick out some matching laundry baskets or hampers. Though you'll want something that works for your family and your laundry system, using similar baskets will give the room a more cohesive look.

🜋 Tuck extra rags out of sight in a big woven basket or bin.

🜋 Bring in texture on the walls or in a cozy rug on the floor.

🜋 Add art and vintage signage on the walls or shelving.

🜋 Create vignettes of useful laundry and cleaning items on shelves or hanging from hooks. I like to buy natural wood or white products, such as scrub brushes, brooms, dusters, or dustpans.

We all know we're going to be spending more than a bit of time in the laundry room, so make it your own cozy, welcoming space.

CREATING A COZY BUTLER'S PANTRY

WINTER
NO.
80
TIP

Our farmhouse didn't have a pantry when we first moved in, but we were able to convert our large laundry space into both a laundry room and a butler's pantry. With a combination of cabinets and countertops, it gives us much-needed storage and frees up space in the kitchen.

Regardless of the size, make the space cozy with thoughtful organizing. Use baskets or bins to corral packages and matching jars or containers for dry goods. The colors of walls, cabinets, and shelving should flow into the surrounding spaces. Even storage can be calming and cozy—especially when things are tidy and easy to find.

COZY PANTRY TIPS

Here are a few options to consider for a kitchen that doesn't have the space for a walk-in butler's pantry:

- Could you add shelving and repurpose a nearby closet?
- Do you have a dining room? Some people close these in and repurpose them. Or it can be a great spot to add an armoire—a thrifted, painted armoire can suddenly become a beautiful pantry.
- Do you have a wide hallway or other nook that would hold some extra shelving or cabinetry? A space-saving trick is to use upper cabinets on both the top and bottom. You can add a counter to fit and still expand both storage and workspace.
- Can you convert the space under your kitchen island for pantry storage? Baskets or drawers can be used to store pantry essentials.

COZY CORRESPONDENCE

Whether it's writing a real, old-fashioned letter, scribbling down an idea before it wanders away, or simply jotting down a grocery list, writing is a part of our everyday lives.

Because writing *is* such a part of our lives, carve out your own cozy space for it. Gather stationery and stamps for letters, pretty papers and pads for list making, journals for reflecting, and planners for keeping everyone and everything in their appointed times and places. Often, I find that the colors, textures, and designs appeal to my senses, keeping me not only on task but inspired. And don't forget the pens and pencils! Pretty, practical, and crazily colorful—I love them all and keep them by the handfuls. Experiment to find your favorites.

It's nice to have a dedicated space for writing. Perhaps it's at a traditional desk in an office, or at a simple table in the corner

of the living room, or maybe it's a basket that can be easily pulled out and sprawled across the dining room table when the creative juices are flowing. With just a bit of intentionality, we can find ways to bring a cozy touch to even the most everyday tasks.

HANDMADE ORNAMENTS

I love making my own ornaments. By making my own, I can get the exact custom look I want. Here are a few examples of my favorites that you can easily create yourself:

Wood ornaments: Visit a craft store and search through their collection of mini wooden cutouts. Leave them undecorated for a rustic look—or stain, paint, or even stamp the wood to achieve the look you want.

Paper cutouts: Use paper to make ornaments or garlands. From paper stamp cutouts to tracing to drawing your own shapes, there are so many paths you can take. Cut shapes out of cardstock or ordinary paper. Finish with paint, glitter, and a ribbon for hanging.

Chunky yarn garland: My favorite way to decorate a tree in an affordable way is to use chunky yarn for garland and ornament ties. Or try pom-pom yarn to add texture to your tree.

Clay shapes: Kids' craft clay is the easiest to use. Once you've shaped your creations, simply poke a hole at the top and let them air dry. Paint or leave as is for a monochromatic look.

CUSTOM COZY GARLANDS

Garlands add so much texture and presence to our décor, whatever the season. But let's face it: finding the perfect garland without breaking the bank can seem like an impossible mission. That's why making your own is such a great option. It's so easy, and you can use faux branches, real branches, or mix them together to create your own gorgeous garland, custom-made to fit your home. To make your own garland, follow these steps:

1. Gather branches, real or faux. You can use a variety of branches, such as firs, pines, spruces, or even magnolias and other types of leaves for a blended, eclectic look. Or grab a smattering of a single type to make a beautiful, full garland that will be the centerpiece of your seasonal spaces.

2. Lay branches all facing the same way and overlapping each other. You can stack them two to three layers deep to create volume and fullness. Secure sections of the branches together with floral wire. Keep in mind, we're not creating an entire length of garland at this point, only sections.

3. Using those small sections, begin adding them—one at a time—to

your mantel, staircase, or other area. Secure them with string, zip ties, 3M strips, or even staples (only in places where the damage won't matter). By working with smaller sections, and not creating the long garland before you hang it, you can manipulate the shape to fit the space you're working with.

4. After the branches are hung, it's time to add in the extras. For example, clip in dried orange slices or pinecones for winter, large floral pieces in spring, lemons in summer, and gourds for fall. Be as creative as you like. Feeling extra festive? Tie loops of ribbon at all the places where the garland is secured to give it a casually draped and effortless look.

GATHER 'ROUND THE CHRISTMAS TREE

The Christmas tree is the focal point of holiday décor and celebrations. And at White Cottage Farm, we don't limit ourselves to just one tree. Rather, we like to spread the cheer throughout our home. We even put one up out in the gazebo for an extra touch of holiday cheer outside. The sizes, shapes, and colors of the trees vary—and sometimes that variety even changes from year to year.

When deciding how to style the tree(s), think of the purpose of the space and who is going to be gathering there, and allow that to inspire how you decorate the tree. I like having multiple trees throughout our home as a way to bring the holiday spirit into each room, creating a festive anchor or focal point to the space.

If you look through the pictures or browse through my blog, you'll notice that I don't often use traditional tree stands and skirts. I like to be a bit more inventive, so instead we'll stand our tree up in a basket,

a bucket, or an oversized planter. Once, we even tucked the base of a small tree inside a vintage suitcase—a look I absolutely loved.

We also put a small tree in our son's room that he helps us decorate each year. The ornaments for his tree are much more colorful and whimsical, just right for his spirit and energy. I know I'm going to love seeing the way it changes over the years, as he grows.

When it comes time to pick out and decorate your tree, be sure to make it your own tree. I personally love a bit of nostalgia—things I can look at and immediately feel the Christmas spirit. If it's vintage ornaments that make you smile and give you all the cozy Christmas vibes, then go for it. If it's sparkly new ornaments, homemade treasures by your kids, or no ornaments at all that says *Merry Christmas* to you, that's wonderful too. Make this Christmas cozy for you and yours.

WHERE TO HANG STOCKINGS

Christmas is coming, and that means Santa is coming . . . and stockings need to be hung. Tradition has us wanting to hang the stockings by the fireplace, but so many of us don't have fireplaces or mantels. So where can those stockings go? Give one of these options a try:

- Hang them along a staircase, using 3M hooks, or stocking holders, or loop them through a garland branch.
- Hook them on the knobs of a dresser.
- Hang them from a shelf or on a row of hooks.
- Attach them to the window using a suction cup hanger.
- Hook them on wreath stands.

CREATE A COZY ADVENT

Advent is a time of anticipation, specifically the weeks leading up to Christmas and the celebration of the birth of Christ. I often use an Advent calendar to serve as a reminder for my family and me to be present each day to the meaning of the season, and you can find a fun DIY project to make your own Advent calendar on LizMarieBlog.com.

During this season of waiting and preparation, it's easy to become distracted by all of the shiny ornaments, the shopping, the wrapping, the shipping, the baking—the *exhaustion*. Instead, consider taking a moment each day during Advent to remember and reflect and take a deep breath. Things don't have to be perfect. But I do like to be intentional.

Other ideas to celebrate the occasion include daily family readings or even creating a simple yet special family gathering early in the season, outside of the traditional Christmas Eve and Day, where there are fewer presents but much more *presence*.

WHITE COTTAGE FARM

LIZ'S COZY COCOA

Start with a basic cocoa mix, add a pinch of sea salt, a dash of cinnamon, and a few dark chocolate chips. Stir in hot water for a sweet and salty twist on an old favorite.

DON'T FORGET

- spoons or stirrers
- marshmallows
- candy canes or crushed peppermint
- sea salt
- cinnamon
- chocolate chips
- a thermal carafe or kettle

No. 87

see more on
LizMarieBlog.com

During the winter months, I like to keep a mini hot chocolate bar set up in a corner of the kitchen. When guests arrive, I can quickly and easily expand this into a full-fledged hot cocoa bar with all the yummy options. I love being able to welcome people into our home by quickly filling their hands with a warm drink and perhaps a snack to tide them over until dinner is served.

I love nesting everything on a bed of evergreen branches. My collection of Santa mugs is both decorative and practical. Make it personal with your own collection or family treasures, whether it's your grandmother's apron or a favorite cookie jar—whatever says cozy and Christmas to you.

STORING SEASONAL DÉCOR

My winter décor takes up most of my seasonal storage. If you're ready to change how you store seasonal décor, begin with a purge. Donate or sell anything you don't love or haven't used in years. Then follow these tips for storing your treasures:

Faux stems and greenery: Lay delicate stems and greenery out in plastic, shallow storage boxes. Or, if space allows, store stems upright in unused vases. Drape with a light sheet to keep dust-free.

Linens: Store throws and pillow covers in vacuum-sealed storage bags that compress to save space. Tuck seasonal tea towels, aprons, napkins, and tablecloths into the drawers of a dresser or stack in an armoire.

Dishes: Seasonal pieces such as Santa cups, Halloween punch bowls, and fall platters can be stored in a butler's pantry or armoire. Felt rounds placed between pieces keep them from chipping. Or wrap pieces carefully and pack into plastic bins.

Wreaths and garlands: Hang in a storage closet or carefully pack into large bins.

Christmas trees: Pack trees into Christmas tree bags (we got ours from Balsam Hill) and then store in the attic.

Ornaments: Carefully wrap and store in partitioned bins.

Rugs and wall hangings: Drape over a hanger, or roll and tuck into a drawer or bin. For larger pieces, roll and cover with a sheet or plastic to keep dust-free.

FUNCTION OVER FORM

Through the wonders of social media, we have access to endless inspiration right at our fingertips. But that can be both a blessing and a curse. Yes, it's a blessing to connect with so many different talented people from near and far who can help us through our decorating woes. Yet that same connection can become a curse when—in an attempt to get just the "right" look—we force ourselves to mimic styles that don't work for us simply because we love the way it looks in someone else's home. We often don't pause to think about how the home functions for that person and their family—and how it might or might not function for ours. We are so inspired by the form of the space that we aren't considering the function.

I'm a little embarrassed to admit that I have made design choices that ended up completely being form over function. I remember one time in particular that still makes me giggle because it caused some

embarrassing moments not only for us, but also for our guests. It was during the height of the barn door craze. I kept seeing them everywhere, and I decided we had to have one on White Cottage Farm. We didn't have many doors that could be replaced at the time, so I hung the barn door up for the guest bathroom, which was right off the kitchen and already didn't offer a ton of privacy. Once in place, that door was gorgeous! But there was just one little problem. On either side of the door was a tiny gap, allowing those outside the bathroom to see (and hear) everything that happened inside. I'd seen barn doors work in so many other people's spaces, so it had to work in ours. Except it didn't. The form was good, but the function was a fail. Eventually, we replaced it, though our family and friends still laugh at our infamous barn door bathroom.

Choosing form over function may give you the look you want, and it may garner you all the likes on social media, but it's the function that is going to make your home cozy for you and your family. That function will look different for every home and family—and that's okay. There is no one perfect way.

Our homes all function in wonderfully different ways. Each of us has our own wants, needs, desires, and goals for the spaces in which we live. And we all have different definitions of cozy. So, yes, keep reading and scrolling and gathering inspiration. But before you shop, tear down, or repaint, ask yourself this: Am I only in love with the form, or will this idea truly function for my home and family?

NO. 90

WINTER TIP

HOW TO STYLE BOOKSHELVES

I'm always tinkering with vignettes and adding new books to my collection. But there are a few guidelines I tend to follow. I love mixing books with everyday utilitarian pieces and my favorite decorative finds.

Start at the bottom and work up, with the "weightiest" pieces placed on the lowest shelves. This is both visually helpful and sometimes necessary and can help stabilize the shelves if your piece is not built in or anchored to the wall. Then add other, larger items, like blankets, cushions, baskets with lids, or bulky containers. These larger pieces are wonderful for hiding cords and plugs. If you have wider shelves, add visual weight to each of the sides as well. I love using bookshelves to group and spotlight my collections, or decorating my shelves with items that are similar in style or color for a cohesive look.

What is a bookshelf without books? Stand them up vertically or stack them horizontally. Arrange them with the spines facing in or out. Remove jackets for a more uniform look.

Style the area around bookshelves with a cozy chair or two and a table to hold a favorite book and beverage. Finish with a footstool, pillows, throws—or whatever makes you feel cozy.

A FEW OF MY FAVORITE THINGS . . .

Sometimes my collections can get a little out of control. Can you relate? My tip is to stick to one color palette within your collections, which can help you pare down if you are running out of space, and it's easier to say no to pieces that don't fit your color scheme.

COZY FIREPLACE IDEAS

WINTER
NO.
91
TIP

When it comes to creating a cozy atmosphere, there's nothing quite like the pop and crackle of a fireplace. Even beyond its obvious uses for warmth and light, fireplaces offer so many opportunities for creative décor.

If you have a real fireplace, you are blessed. Here at the farm, we don't have a working, wood-burning fireplace. But we re-create the cozy effect by wrapping the logs in twinkle lights or placing faux candles in them for a glow without the flames. This is also a good option if you don't enjoy building fires, or if an active and curious toddler makes you nervous about lighting a large fire.

Electric fireplaces are also a possibility. There is an endless variety of them, from standalone pieces that resemble vintage stoves to sleeker ones that are built into the walls. There are models that come with mantels, but if you love a good DIY, you can build your own, or incorporate an antique mantel with an electric fireplace.

And speaking of mantels . . . every season brings with it the chance to style these beauties with garlands and greenery, art prints and vintage pieces, favorite family photos, candles—whatever your cozy heart desires. You don't even have to have a fireplace to incorporate a mantel into your décor, which is what we've done in our front room. To fill in the "hole" under the mantel, choose a large plant, add baskets of seasonal stems, or simply leave it empty to show the space behind.

Do you have a chilly space that would benefit from the beauty and warmth of a fireplace? As you take stock of your winter décor, consider incorporating a cozy fireplace or mantel in your home.

WINTER
NO.
92
TIP

COZY HIBERNATION

Winter can be quite tough, and I don't just mean because of all the snow and ice. To be perfectly honest, the winter blues are a struggle for me. I so love the outdoors that it's difficult to stay inside and keep motivated. So I've tried to change my way of thinking about these winter months. Instead of being "stuck" inside, I'm choosing to think of it as a cozy hibernation.

Winter is naturally the season of rest, not just for the land and the trees but also for us. So on cold, dreary days, I give myself permission to do just that. Rest. Sometimes I struggle to accept this, but it's something that both my body and my soul need. It's something we all need. I try to be intentional during this season of short, cloudy days and long nights.

What does winter rest look like? We still have kids and jobs and things to do, but we can incorporate meaningful rhythms into our days to help us cultivate rest and refresh our souls. Here's my winter rest list:

- Start a new morning ritual to wake up your body, such as stretching or yoga.
- Carve out some time in your day for journaling, praying, or meditating.
- Enjoy a hot cup of coffee or tea in blessed silence before your day begins.
- Put a jar of your favorite bath salts by the tub and indulge in a warm winter bath.
- Go to bed early.

When my spirits need a refresh, sometimes I just pull on my softest sweater, scoop up Cope, and wrap us up in our favorite blanket to read a book and sip hot cocoa. These are the days for taking time to be a little leisurely, resting our minds and bodies, and loving our people. And that's a good thing. So tell me, how do you hibernate?

The entryway is more than just a way to enter a house. This is your opportunity to welcome guests into your home and to welcome yourself and your loved ones back home. It should be not only appealing to the eyes but also practical—both for us and for our guests. And, of course, it must be cozy. In winter, at least in Michigan, we're often dealing with snow. So, the entryway must also be able to comfortably handle the wet as well as all the bulky items needed for life in the cold.

Because entryways are usually small spaces, make sure everything in it is functional and works for you. I love to start with a vintage bench or lockers. It's not only cozy but so practical as a spot to put on boots and shoes and then take them off again. Tuck a boot tray underneath to keep floors tidy. If your space doesn't allow for a bench or set of lockers, consider a small chair or stool.

Next, add hooks for hanging up coats, scarves, and other snow gear. Authentic vintage hooks are my absolute favorite, and I add to my collection whenever I can. Look for them at flea markets, on eBay, or on Etsy. Once the functional foundation is laid, it's time to add the cozy. Toss pillows on the bench. Add a basket or market bag for holding mittens, hats, and gloves. Hang art prints and add all the cozy touches that greet you with a warm "Welcome home."

A TOUCH OF WELCOME

One of my very favorite things I've ever had in my entryway is a vintage-inspired log-book I found a few years after we moved to the farm. We welcomed family, friends, and guests to sign it or write a little note about the visit. I have notes from my grandmother and loved ones, and these little moments and notes mean so much to us! I encourage everyone to find a fun little cohesive logbook or notebook to capture these memories for you and your family.

CREATING COZY WITH PETS

Our pets are part of the family, and we believe it's our duty to make them feel that they belong. That means we make our home cozy for them too, with pet beds, cozy crates, and their own areas for curling up in. Because whether or not you allow your pets on the furniture, it's so important for them to have their own cozy spaces where they can relax and feel safe and loved.

At White Cottage Farm, we let our pets up on the furniture. Our dogs love to sleep in our bed and lounge on our sofa with us. This might come as a shock considering we have mostly white furniture in our house! To keep the muddy pawprints from getting everywhere, we've developed a routine that allows our pets to get clean before they run through the house. After being outside, they stay and relax in the mudroom until they have dried off and are clean. If you don't have a mudroom, consider gating off your kitchen or entryway to keep pets contained until you're ready for them to roam the house.

Even with this system in place, our pets create messes. That's just what pets do. Keep the mess to a minimum with pet-friendly furniture. Our sofas and chairs are slipcovered for easy cleaning. To stretch out the time between washings, we cover them with blankets, so our furry friends are welcome to jump up anytime. And while our white wooden floors might look difficult to keep clean, they are the definition of low-maintenance. A quick sweep and they practically look like new again.

If you've welcomed a pet into your heart and home, give some thought as to how you can make sure that they're cozy too.

THE WHITE COTTAGE FARM

MY PET ESSENTIALS

- Rug or doormat at their door of entry.
- Mudroom or gate to let them have some "drying time."
- Extra blankets to toss over furniture they like to get on. (Thrift for blankets or quilts in your color scheme for a low-cost option.)
- Their own cozy beds.

No. 94

see more on
LizMarieBlog.com

COZY HOLIDAY CARD DISPLAY

I love sending and receiving Christmas cards. It's so wonderful to hear from friends and family across the miles and see their updated family pictures. And once the cards start piling in, the colorful collection can become its own festive display.

I like to use unique pieces for backdrops, and in this case I used an old toboggan and hung the cards with magnets. What's great about large pieces like this one is that it fills an otherwise empty corner. And for the rest of the year, if I choose to keep this piece in place, I can collect other greeting cards, postcards, and letters to display and remind me of my loved ones.

Here are some suggestions for displaying holiday cards this season:

- Find a vintage sled or toboggan like ours and use it as a backdrop.

- Set up a pair of crisscrossed skis, new or vintage, and attach the cards to the skis.

- Use reclaimed windows or cabinet doors with leaded glass panes to hold your collection.

- Hang a piece of garland wrapped with white lights across a wall or doorframe, or along a bannister, and use clothespins to attach cards.

- For a more rustic look, use twine with clothespins instead of garland.

- If you tend to have a smaller and sweeter array, find a piece of driftwood and hang the cards from fishing line or thin ribbon with gallery clips tied to the ends.

- Slot the cards behind and among a generous display of greenery, lights, and ribbon across a fireplace mantel or bookshelf.

INDOOR HERB GARDEN

If you haven't noticed by now, I love plants and gardening. Sadly, our Michigan winters don't allow for much outdoor vegetable gardening, but indoors is a great opportunity for growing edibles for your family. While you can grow herbs indoors year-round, winter is a perfect time to keep your thumbs green and your gardener soul happy.

Don't be afraid to get a little wild here. Too often, we see the tiny, petite, adorable herb gardens—often three little pots in a picture-perfect windowsill. Depending on what herbs you use regularly, consider going big. Why not grow huge rosemary or lavender bushes in oversized containers? This not only serves your culinary purposes but also can add extra coziness to kitchens or really anywhere. Not to mention, they add a beautiful aroma, especially when freshly snipped for dinner.

Here are some terrific, oversized herbs to grow indoors.

WHITE COTTAGE FARM

INDOOR HERB GARDEN

	Chives				
	Cilantro				
	Giant Italian parsley				
	Greek oregano				
	Large leaf Italian basil				
	Lavender				
	Lemon balm				
	Mint				
	Parsley				
	Rosemary				
	Sage				
	Thyme				

No. 96

see more on
LizMarieBlog.com

WINTER SEEDS STARTERS

Don't forget to start your seeds during late winter! Remember to check your planting zone to ensure successful crops. Some of the commercial seed trays can get messy and take up a lot of room. Unless you have a good place out of the way to keep them, they can become an eyesore. Consider starting seeds in the following containers to add cute, cozy touches and to keep watchful eyes in your main areas. This is also a great way to upcycle some items and reduce waste.

- Cardboard egg cartons
- Mason jars
- Old muffin tins
- Tin cans with their food labels removed
- Used K-cups lined up on a serving tray
- Newspapers rolled and folded into little seed cups organized on a shallow tray

WINTER
NO.
97
TIP

A COZY NEW YEAR'S EVE

The hustle and bustle of the holidays have quieted, and at the end of the year, I feel a sense of calm and completion. In fact, one of the things we like to do for New Year's Eve is reflect on the past year, remembering everything we've accomplished, relishing some of those special memories, celebrations, and bucket-list outings that bring us so much joy each year.

To honor this time, I'll keep this one simple. Take time to reflect on all the goals you accomplished and note the ones you might choose to complete in the coming year. Give yourself grace for those things you didn't complete. There's a saying, "We're either winning, or we're learning." Either share this idea with a loved one, or simply write this to yourself in a journal.

At the year's end, ask:

What did I do well?

What challenges did I overcome?

What did I learn?

What am I letting go of?

And then do just that. Let go, relax, and enjoy, for a new day is coming!

Add these special touches for an at-home cozy New Year's Eve, perfect for just one or many:

- Twinkling white lights or candles
- Your best stemware or glassware, polished to reflect the light
- Something bubbly, garnished with fresh berries or fresh herbs
- Your favorite music softly playing in the background
- A clock you love (I have a whole collection) to help count down to the brand-new year with its blank canvas, just waiting for you to create your dreams

WINTER
NO.
98
TIP

COZY PLANNING DAY

Oh, that glorious feeling of the first day of the new year. The *ultimate* fresh start. You want to relish that moment of newness, and you are almost too scared to do too much for fear of muddying up the new year early on. I love to start the year off slowly without putting tons of pressure on myself or the new year ahead. Many start the year off with a long list of goals, but I love starting the new year with a cozy planning day. No high expectations, just a cup of tea, a pen, a binder full of blank sheets, and an open mind. Of course, you can do this any day of the year and in any season, but the first day of the new year is a great day to implement some cozy plans.

I've listed some ideas to help you get started with your own cozy planning day where you can begin to look forward to the exciting year ahead!

SOME THINGS TO LOOK FORWARD TO:

- Make a mood board or vision board.
- Make a wish list.
- Plan your garden and house goals.
- Plan for time off and vacations.
- Make your seasonal bucket lists, including celebrations and outings.
- Be sure to set dates on your calendar as reminders of the fun things to look forward to!
- Make a list of home projects you want to tackle.
- Plan your family vacations and staycations.
- Make a list of purchases you want to make throughout the year or things you need to buy for your home renovations.
- Write out your "why" with a list of your purposes, values, and any changes you want to make.
- Journal your New Year's resolutions, your goals, or your word of the year.

MY COZY VALENTINE

I tend to take a minimalist approach to Valentine's Day, though if you like a bolder splash, I hope you take these ideas and spice them up to make them your own. Here are two of my favorite Valentine touches.

GROCERY-STORE FLOWERS

Yes, you read that correctly. I love to get a big armload of grocery-store flowers and spread them throughout the house in several unique vases or put them all in one giant bouquet. Here are my favorite flower tips:

- Not all grocery-store flowers are created equal. As grocers are a very regional thing, be sure to check the flower sections of the stores you frequent to see which carries the best blooms.
- Don't forget the greens. Sometimes a flowers-only bouquet can pack a perfect punch, but if you want to create something large with a lot of visual interest, buy stems of separate greens. Taking the leaves off of flower stems can help the flowers last longer, so it's great to have separate green stems to show off foliage.
- You know I love a unique vase or an old, chippy pot. Whether you make many small bouquets or one large one, find something really original to feature your flowers.
- Mix it up or go monochrome. This is completely dependent on my mood of the day. Are you feeling colorful and festive, or do you want to stick with one color scheme?

PAPER HEART GARLAND

A simple string of white paper hearts, paired with fresh flowers, is just enough Valentine décor for me, but you might want to show off some vibrant reds or pinks to go with it. If you're not feeling crafty, you

220

can order all manner of heart garlands online. Here are a few paper-heart tips if you want an easy, DIY craft:

- ❦ As you probably know, I love to stick with whites and simple neutrals. One way to add interest is to make your hearts out of old book or music pages or interesting white craft paper patterns.

- ❦ You can use a Cricut to cut out your hearts or freehand this simple shape. If you want to create a 3D image, simply cut strips of paper at varying lengths and connect the tops and bottoms of your hearts with a staple. Add ribbon, twine, or kitchen string, and . . .

- ❦ Voilà! Drape your hearts and place your flowers around the house for a simple but lovely Valentine's Day. For the coziest of days, shower your loved ones with hugs, snuggles, and favorite yummy treats.

THERE ARE NO RULES

There are no rules. Let's say that again and let it really sink in. There are no rules. Literally none. At least not when it comes to creating a cozy home for you and your family.

In a world where so many of us are raising our kids, sometimes homeschooling too, working full-time jobs, and trying to create cozy, comfortable homes, things just aren't always going to be perfect. Or the best. I had a major mindset shift one day when I got an unexpected compliment on something I had never really articulated before. This person told me I was doing a wonderful job creating an environment for our child to thrive in. Wow. Wasn't that my main goal all along?

Most of us will never be the biggest or the best when measured against the rest of the world. But all of those things are okay as long as we keep our focus on what matters. I have plenty of parenting fears and worries about things I may not be able to teach or do as well as I would like, but the thing I know is this: I can create a cozy, loving home for my family. I can create an environment for our child to be safe, to grow, and to thrive. And I can use what I've learned to teach others to do the same for themselves and their families.

Cozy isn't about rules. It's about what you love, what you find beautiful, and what works for you and your family. My best cozy tip to you is this: Don't pressure yourself to be the best. Don't compare yourself to what you see on social media. We don't need to struggle against making things beautiful for other peoples' standards—we can simply focus on what makes our homes feel cozy and functional to us. And then do our very best to be present and soak up every cozy moment we can.

From our home to yours,

ACKNOWLEDGMENTS

Thank you so much for picking up this copy of *Cozy White Cottage Seasons*. It was written, curated, and crafted with love from our cozy white cottage farmhouse in Michigan during a difficult year. The trials during this time inspired me to keep this book simple and approachable, because if 2020 taught me anything, it's that cozy spaces are gifts that I will never take for granted. Though we may have differing definitions of cozy, I hope this book inspired you to make your own home cozy no matter the season or circumstance. Thank you again for reading, and thank you to everyone who made this book possible.

Jose, for being the most patient, creative, supportive, and encouraging partner a girl could ask for.

Anna, for spending so much time with me photographing our farmhouse in all its unfinished glory.

Makenzie, for helping with all of my edits. It was a lot and I'm thankful for all you did!

Thank you to the HarperCollins team for having faith in me to write a second book.

Thank you to my manager, Brian, for putting up with my lateness to jobs because of the book writing. He's the real MVP.

Thank you to my blog readers and those who follow me on social media daily. You encourage and inspire me to keep sharing my passions, and I'm forever grateful for you.

Thank you to Tama for helping me get my words out onto paper. You are the greatest!

Thank you to Diane, Pierson, Rose, Tom, Mom, Dad, Matt, and the rest of our village who keeps us going during crazy times and dealing with our busy schedules.

Thank you to Spring Sweet for helping me bring seasonal fun to this book.

Winnie, for being the coziest dog ever and for gracing my book cover once again.

ABOUT THE AUTHOR

Liz Marie Galvan is an author, blogger, momma, wife, and co-owner of the home décor boutique, The Found Cottage. Liz blogs daily on her website, LizMarieBlog.com, where thousands of people go for tips and inspiration each day—whether she's blogging about life on the farm, their fixer-upper 1800s farmhouse, her latest DIY project, or even about their adoption journey. Liz lives in Michigan with her veteran husband, Jose, and their son, Copeland Beau, along with a few sheep, a lot of bees, a bunch of cats, and even a couple of dogs. You can follow Liz and all of her adventures on Instagram @LizMarieGalvan.